# Keto Cooking

*with Your*

# Instant Pot®

# Keto Cooking

### with Your

# Instant Pot®

### Recipes for Fast and Flavorful
### Ketogenic Meals

# Dr. Karen S. Lee
Author of *Paleo Cooking with Your Air Fryer*

PAGE STREET
PUBLISHING CO.

PAGE STREET
PUBLISHING CO.

First published in 2019 by
Page Street Publishing Co.
27 Congress Street, Suite 105
Salem, MA 01970
www.pagestreetpublishing.com

Distributed by Macmillan, sales in Canada by The Canadian Manda Group.

23  22  21 20  19     3  4  5  6  7

ISBN-13: 978-1-62414-697-8
ISBN-10: 1-62414-697-X

Library of Congress Control Number: 2018952829

Cover and book design by Meg Baskis for Page Street Publishing Co.
Photography by Donna Crous

Printed and bound in the United States

The author of this book has decided that a portion of her proceeds from this book will be donated to the Hudson Valley, New York chapter of Make-A-Wish Foundation®.

Instant Pot® is a registered trademark of Double Insiger, Inc., which was not involved in the creation of this book.

This book is dedicated to Johnson, Bianca, Laurie, Simon and anyone else who has had profound health challenges. Your passion for vitality and purposeful life is truly inspirational despite the difficulties you've endured. I hope this book will help you continue to thrive, conquer and enjoy every step of your life's journey.

*"Let food be thy medicine and medicine be thy food."* —Socrates

# Introduction

There are many reasons why people start the Ketogenic diet. Initially, the Ketogenic (or Keto) diet was mainly used to control epileptic seizures in patients in the 1920s. Since then, it has been shown to help those with diabetes, cancer, cardiovascular health issues and obesity. As for my family, we began the Ketogenic journey to control inflammation and weight gain. Since my goal in the kitchen is to make cooking as simple as I can, I use the Instant Pot to cook my family's favorite recipes. *Keto Cooking with Your Instant Pot*® is a collection of our family's favorite Keto recipes that I know you will also enjoy.

I started cooking Paleo-friendly foods for my family a few years ago due to their food allergies. We rarely ate processed foods or the typical Standard American Diet (SAD) to begin with, so it was a natural transition into the Paleo style of eating. But then, my children still had to watch the sugar-induced inflammation, which manifested as eczema, and my husband and I needed to watch our middle-aged bellies. So, I decided to add Keto meals to our already clean eating style. To my surprise, it has been a really easy transition to a no-added-sugar diet, and the results have been amazing. My kids' skin looks healthy and vibrant, with no redness or irritation. My husband and I are enjoying eating delicious foods without guilt. No matter what stage of the Keto diet you're on, these recipes will help you stay satiated and satisfied—they did for my family!

Important reminder: If you are on the Keto diet to lose weight, it's important to find out what is causing the weight gain to begin with. Hormones, stress, sedentary lifestyle, side effects of medication and inflammation—to name a few—can cause weight gain. So, while reducing sugar intake is always a good idea in general since sugar causes inflammation, if you are thinking of starting the Keto diet to lose weight, you should first find out if there are any other underlying medical conditions causing your weight gain.

I also want to point out that the Keto diet is not just another fad diet for weight loss. The Keto diet is a healthy lifestyle of eating great-tasting whole foods in controlled portions. More importantly, the Keto diet means eating home-cooked meals as often as you can, so you can control what goes into your food. While it may be convenient to eat prepared foods labeled "low-carb" or "sugar-free," there might be potentially harmful chemicals that make the foods that way. Also, some processed food contains hidden carbs you might not notice.

Artificial or natural sweeteners can still spike insulin responses, even if they don't contain carbs, not to mention cause intestinal problems for many people. Moreover, prepared food containers can contain hormone-disrupting chemicals like BPA and phthalate that can cause weight gain.

So, in this book, you won't find anything packaged or processed, but only fresh and whole ingredients. The goal is not only to make easy home-cooked meals, but also to cook nourishing foods with rich flavors that only fresh ingredients can deliver.

On a personal note, when I started the Keto diet, I didn't even have to exercise for the weight to come off. Now, this doesn't mean you shouldn't exercise. Physical activity is important for cardiovascular health, so that's not negotiable. But the point is, you can exercise all you want, but if you are still eating carb-heavy foods, the weight is not going to come off. Hopefully, this collection of low-carb, real, wholesome recipes you can cook in the Instant Pot will help you get started.

I first heard about the Instant Pot through blogs and social media. I thought it was just another cooking gadget that was bound to eventually wind up collecting dust on my kitchen counter. To my delight, the Instant Pot turned out to be so much more than a pressure cooker. I use it weekly to cook just about everything now. It has replaced my slow cooker, rice cooker, roaster and stove-top pressure cooker. I have the assurance that I'm serving my family healthy food cooked in a safe appliance without toxic chemicals, and I've decluttered my kitchen at the same time.

With the Instant Pot, it's so much easier to make meals that used to take hours, like rib roast, Osso Buco, Bouef Bourguignon and Korean-style short ribs. I'd have to watch the simmering pot on the stove all day whenever I made bone broth, but now it only takes a few hours and I don't have to watch the pot! Making nourishing soups like classic chicken soup, clam chowder, *cioppino* and *zuppa Toscana* is a cinch, and comforting stews like beef stew and chili con carne are a breeze. It even makes desserts like cheesecake and lava cake!

My goal in writing this book was to help you cook nourishing foods easily in the Instant Pot, so that you can face your unique health challenges using common ingredients that you probably already have. And if you don't have them, you can easily find them at your local grocery stores, if not on Amazon. So, for all you busy cooks out there struggling to put low-carb and healthy whole foods on the table, this book is dedicated to you. Being on the Keto diet is challenging enough; cooking doesn't have to be stressful when you can use the Instant Pot to make your favorite dishes without fail. The fresh, wholesome ingredients are so good that you won't even notice they're low-carb!


In Your Health!

*Dr. Karen*

# Tips for Using the Instant Pot

Over a million people own the Instant Pot, and there are good reasons why they do. The Instant Pot makes delicious tender foods and cooks faster, and easy cooking makes busy families eat healthier meals at home more often. But, like many things in life, there are some guidelines you should remember to optimize your experience.

1.  **Read the Manual**—I know that sounds obvious, but answers to many of your questions can be found in the manual, especially about your model. This cookbook is written with generic instructions for the cooking time and pressure settings, regardless of the model. But if you are looking for model–specific answers, refer to the manual. Before cooking anything in the Instant Pot, perform the "Initial Test Run" according to the instructions in the manual to ensure the cooker is functioning properly.

2.  **Cooking Times**—Cooking times that you see on pressure cooker recipes, including those in this book, are always the actual cooking times under pressure and on "Sauté" (if using.) Pressure cooking times in recipes do not include the time to pressurize or to de-pressurize, similar to recipes that do not include time to preheat the oven or the time it takes to reach proper temperature on the stove. So, be mindful of "Cooking Time" in pressure cooker recipes since it's not the "Total Time" from beginning to end of cooking. You can always change the cooking time to "Less," "Normal" or "More" or use the "+" or "−" buttons to reach the desired temperature. Also, cooking times are for altitudes around 2000 feet (609.6 m) above sea level and lower. For every 1000 feet (304.8 m) above 2000 feet (609.6 m), add 5 percent to the cooking times.

3.  **Cooking Frozen Foods**—One of the benefits of using the Instant Pot is cooking at the last minute when you forget to defrost your meals or meats. One of the few tricks I learned in making successful meals from the freezer is to always season the meat before freezing. This way, it's always perfectly seasoned when you take it out of the freezer! Also, remember to freeze any prepared meals or meats in round shapes and sizes that can fit in the inner pot. This way, you can take them out of the container and place them in the inner pot without defrosting. Frozen meats take 5 to 10 percent longer to cook but do not need any extra liquid other than what the recipe calls for.

4.  **Times to Pressure and to De-Pressurize**—For pressure cooking, the time to pressurize or to de-pressurize depends on the amount of liquid, food, fat content and altitude. Dishes with more liquid or food, or higher fat content or altitude, require a longer time to pressurize. Also, a cold cooker takes longer than a warm cooker. Normally, a cold cooker takes about 10 minutes to pressurize (10 to 20 minutes for a full pot) and 10 to 20 minutes to depressurize (can take up to 40 minutes for a full pot), depending on what you're cooking. One trick to make a cooker pressurize faster is to put it on the "Sauté" function to heat it up and then use the pressure cooker function.

5. **Timer Screen**—Ten seconds after the timer for the Instant Pot is set, the cooker beeps 3 times and displays "ON." The cooker builds pressure during this time and when it pressurizes, the screen changes to the set time, i.e., 00:10 for 10 minutes. As the cooker cooks, the number counts DOWN. When the cooking time finishes and the cooker beeps, it automatically switches to the "Keep Warm" setting. The timer goes back to 00:00 (or L0:00 on some models) and the number counts UP to indicate the amount of time it stays under "Keep Warm." Depending on the model, this setting can be from 10 to 24 hours. If the recipe indicates to move the steam release handle to release pressure manually (QR), this is the time to do so. You can also turn OFF the cooker by pressing the "Cancel" button at any time.

6. **A Minimum Amount of Liquid**—The Instant Pot needs at least ½ cup (120 ml) to 1 cup (240 ml) of liquid to pressurize. Cooking food that requires a long time, like a 4-pound (1.8-kg) pot roast, requires at least 1 cup (240 ml) of liquid, whereas vegetables take "0" minutes, so they need only ½ cup (120 ml) of liquid. Also, dense foods like meat needs at least 1 cup (240 ml) of liquid, whereas foods with higher water content require less liquid since its water content evaporates and creates more water.

7. **Multi-Function Buttons**—Instant Pot prides itself on its multi-functionality, and the preprogrammed buttons are on the panel for your convenience. But, they can be confusing at first. To simplify, except for "Slow Cooker," "Sauté" and "Yogurt," all of the functions are pressure cooking functions and will need the Instant Pot lid. And all of the pressure cooking functions are on HIGH pressure, except for "Rice." They are all preprogrammed for different pressure cooking options but remember, those are just general guidelines. The models made after Duo-60 will remember your last preferred pre-programmed settings. Unfortunately, these settings may be different for different models, so always check to make sure the cook times or "Mode" indicators are correctly set for the recipes you are making. This cookbook does NOT use any of the pre–programmed buttons to avoid confusion for readers with different models. Instead, I've specified the exact cook time and pressure in each recipe, so regardless of which model you have, you can refer to the instructions.

8. **QR (Quick Release)**—This term literally means quickly releasing the pressure manually by turning the steam release handle on the top of the lid to the "Opening" position. This method is used for vegetables, non-foaming foods and in cases where the food's texture is not an issue, like with soup. This method is also used to add ingredients in the middle of cooking—i.e., adding vegetables for Beef Stew—and then continuing to cook until done. But it's important to remember to only use this method if your pot is NOT filled up to the Max line to prevent food from sputtering through the steam release handle or through the float valve. NEVER cover the steam release handle or the float valve when releasing pressure; it could break the cooker. Using tongs, turn the steam release handle slowly, away from your body, and close it quickly if you see sputtering food. To avoid this, open it little at a time until the pressure is fully released.

9. **NPR (Natural Pressure Release)**—This term refers to letting the pressure release naturally as the cooker cools down. After the timer ends, and the cooker beeps, the cooker cools down under the "Warm" setting and it releases the pressure by itself. You can open the lid when the float valve drops down. This setting is used almost always for tender meats, foamy foods and a full pot of food that's filled up to the Max line. Some recipes call for "10 NPR," which means release the pressure manually 10 minutes after it switches to the "Keep Warm" setting. The panel should say "00:10." Again, release the pressure a little at time and avoid being in front of the steam.

10. **Steam Release Handle**—Devise a system to remember to turn the handle to "Sealing" position when you start the cooker. Trust me, you will forget at least once and the first time you hear the hissing sound of pressure releasing prematurely will make you nervous that your meal is ruined. If that happens, just move the handle to "Sealing" position and the cooker will continue to cook as planned. But develop a routine to always put the handle on "Sealing" position before walking away.

11. **Float Valve**—Normally, the float valve will pop up when the cooker reaches pressure and drops down when the cooker is de-pressurized. If the float valve does not pop up but the cooker is hot, it may be because: 1. There isn't enough food or liquid in the cooker and 2. The silicone ring is loose and the lid is not sealed completely. If the first situation is the reason, don't worry, the cooker is still hot and your food will be cooked eventually. Open the pot and check to see if the food is done. If the food is not cooked, add more water or food. Close the lid and try again. The second situation can happen if the cooker was cooking food for too long—i.e., bone broth for 4 hours—and the cooker is being used again. Using the cooker for a long period of time under pressure makes the silicone ring stretch out, so the lid will not close tightly and steam will escape. To shrink the silicone ring to fit the lid correctly, run it under cold water or put it in the freezer for 10 minutes before using it again. You can also use a new silicone sealing ring.

12. **Maintenance**—Wash the inner pot, lid and the silicone ring each time after you cook, either by hand or in the dishwasher. Washing them after each use will keep the smell out of the lid and the silicone ring, especially after cooking pungent recipes like Classic Bone Broth (page 30) or Better Butter Chicken (page 129). Also, clean out any food particles that might be stuck in between the silicone ring and the lid. Thoroughly cleaning the lid and the silicone ring regularly will prevent any possible malfunctions, i.e., not reaching pressure, the lid not sealing completely and unwanted odor. For convenience, have an extra silicone ring for mild-tasting foods like Espresso Mocha Cheesecake (page 168) or Immune-Boosting Ginger Tea (page 179). Besides, cooking with two rings will prevent overuse of one ring, which may cause it to stretch out and not seal the cooker properly.

13. **Other Instant Pot Mysteries**—Usually, there should not be a lot of steam coming out of the cooker, but if you see steam coming out of the float valve or through the steam release handle, don't panic. It's normal to see some steam escaping until the cooker comes to pressure and the float valve goes up to seal it completely. But if the steam continues to escape through the float valve, steam release handle or even from the sides of the lid and the cooker is NOT pressurizing, make sure the steam release handle is in the "Sealing" position. If it is, then open the lid and check to make sure the silicone ring is in place properly and there are no food particles within the perimeter of the lid holding the sealing ring in place. Also make sure there are no food particles in the float valve hole. Close the lid tightly and gently lift the lid up and push down. Sometimes a gentle nudge from an outside force can create a seal and pressurize the cooker.

14. **Instant Pot Sizes**—I used Instant Pot Duo60—6 Quart (5.7 L)—to write this cookbook. If you have a different size cooker, adjust the ingredient amounts to fit your cooker's size. Except for soups that require 5 cups (1.2 L) of liquid or large size meats, you should not have any issues with the ingredient amounts in this cookbook. If you want smaller portions, make the recipe as written and freeze any leftovers since Instant Pot is great for reheating frozen food. Also, I stated actual "Cooking Times" instead of using preprogrammed buttons, as different models have different settings. Use whichever method you are familiar with in choosing the correct cooking times on your cooker.

# Tips On Using This Cookbook For Your Ketogenic Diet

When you are on the Ketogenic diet, your daily macro may look something like:

- 5–10% of calories from carbs—20–30 grams of net carbs (Total Carbs minus Dietary Fiber)

- 15–30% of calories from protein

- 60–75% calories from fat

Depending on what type of Ketogenic diet you are on, the macro count requirements may be different for you. Here are some of the most common ketogenic diets and their carb counts:

- **Standard Ketogenic Diet (SKD)**—20–50 grams of net carbs per day.

- **Targeted Ketogenic Diet (TKD)**—25–50 grams of net carbs per day with an intake of carbs right before exercise and high-protein and low fat foods after exercise.

- **Carb Loading or Cycling**—50 grams and under—you stick to less than 50 grams of total carbs per day on most days and on some days, you go up as high as 150 grams for fitness, hormone balance or other health reasons.

- **Strict Keto**—20 grams and under—if you are on this strict diet of 20 grams of total carbs per day for clinical reasons, use the recipes that include animal proteins, vegetables that are grown above ground, limited nuts and seeds and berries.

- **Moderate Keto or Keto Reset**—this is a two-step process—the first of which is a slow transitional phase where you train your body to burn fat for fuel instead of carbs. And once this is achieved, you can settle into a stricter Keto diet. This may take 21 to 30 days of eliminating all added sugars, refined grains and some starchy foods like bread and pasta.

I wrote this book to share recipes that my family enjoys while on the Moderate Keto diet, and most of the recipes contain less than 10 grams of total carbs per serving while others are higher. These recipes worked for us, but here are some tips on how to use these recipes to fit your needs.

- **Macro Calculation:** I used numerous sites and apps to calculate the macros and checked them several times for accuracy. Still, these numbers might be different based on the methods you're using. Remember these numbers are just guidelines. Do your own calculations, but more importantly, see how certain ingredients affect you. It's not really about the numbers; it's more about the quality of the ingredients and how they affect your body.

- **Ingredients:** To enhance flavors without using packaged seasonings, I use mostly fresh spices and herbs in my recipes. But I understand that for some people, even fresh ingredients can cause problems. For example, I use fresh garlic and onions, but if you can't tolerate the carb content then use powders.

- **Serving Portions and Sizes:** In my opinion, serving portions are personal. I know there are "recommended" portions per serving, but everyone's needs and preferences are different. The serving sizes per recipe in this book are generous, so adjust the portions to fit your needs. If the total carb count is too high for you, reduce the portion size, thereby increasing the number of servings for the recipe. Many of the recipes make enough for leftovers to freeze for later.

- **Thickeners:** There are a couple of recipes that use a little bit of tapioca flour to thicken sauces and gravy. For some people, this may cause spikes in the glucose levels, so avoid using it if this is a problem for you. But if tapioca flour does not cause problems for you, it's a better thickener than grain flours.

- **Sweeteners:** I don't use sweeteners in these recipes except for in a few desserts. I think natural sweetness from vegetables are better for you than even calorie-free Keto-friendly sweeteners. But if you can't eat carrots or even parsnips, then you can skip them in the recipes.

- **Alcohol:** I don't worry about the carb content in alcohol since we are not big drinkers, but I do use a little bit of extra dry wine for cooking since much of the calorie content is burned off during cooking. Still, if you have issues with alcohol in cooking, you can leave it out entirely. It won't ruin the recipe.

# Breakfasts of Champions

My philosophy on breakfast is to start the day right by eating foods that fuel the body. That means energizing proteins and fats, not sugary cereals or grains that can spike your blood sugar level. It also means to stay away from sweeteners of any kind, even the "natural" sugar substitutes, so your body doesn't trigger an insulin response and then crash an hour later.

Breakfasts with protein and healthy oils and fats, like Eggs en Cocotte (page 18) or classic Bacon, Egg and Cheese Cups (page 21) are simple to make in the Instant Pot. Don't have time to cook in the morning? Make Hard-Boiled Eggs (page 26 for Eggs Three Ways), Low-Carb Nutty Porridge (page 25) or Slow-Cooked Granola On-the-Go (page 22) in advance, and you'll be ready to rock the day without the morning rush!

# Eggs en Cocotte

The first time I read the name of this recipe, I thought it was some fancy French dish. It turns out, it's basically baked eggs with added French flair. It sounds chic and it's easy to make, especially in the Instant Pot. And frankly, everyone should start the day with this fancy but easy breakfast.

*Cook Time: 9 minutes // Servings: 4*

2 tbsp (30 g) unsalted butter, divided

½ cup (40 g) uncured bacon, diced

⅓ cup (53 g) finely diced shallots

⅓ cup (10 g) chopped spinach, leaves only

Pinch of sea salt

Pinch of black pepper

½ cup (120 ml) water

¼ cup (60 ml) heavy whipping cream

8 large eggs

1 tbsp (3 g) chopped fresh chives, for garnish

Turn the Instant Pot on by pressing "Sauté." Melt 1 tablespoon (14.5 g) of butter in the inner pot. Add the bacon and sauté for about 4 minutes until crispy. Using a slotted spoon, take out the bacon bits and place into a bowl and set aside. Add the remaining butter and shallots to the inner pot and sauté for about 2 minutes or until soft. Add the spinach leaves and sauté for 1 minute or until wilted. Sprinkle with pinches of sea salt and black pepper and stir. Take the spinach out and place it into a bowl and set aside. Hit the "Cancel" button.

Drain the oil from the inner pot into a bowl, and put the water and the trivet inside.

With a paper towel, coat four 4-ounce (135 ml) ramekins with the bacon grease. In each ramekin, place 1 tablespoon (15 ml) of heavy whipping cream, reserved bacon bits and sautéed spinach. Carefully, crack two eggs without breaking the yolks in each ramekin. Cover the ramekins with aluminum foil. Place two ramekins on the trivet and stack the other two on top. Press the "Pressure Cooker/Manual" button and set the timer for 2 minutes on LOW pressure. This setting will cook the eggs to be runny. If you'd like firmer whites and yolks, use 2 minutes under HIGH pressure or 4 minutes under LOW pressure.

Close the lid tightly and move the steam release handle to "Sealing." When you hear the beeping sound indicating that the time has ended, carefully turn the steam release handle to the "Venting" position for the steam to escape and the float valve to drop down. Press "Cancel." Open the lid. Carefully take out the ramekins, garnish with the chives and serve immediately.

*Nutrition:* Per Serving: 321 calories; 26g fat; 17g protein; 4g total total carbohydrate; trace dietary fiber

# Bacon, Egg and Cheese Cups

Bacon, egg and cheese on a roll is a quintessential American breakfast sandwich. But since bread is off the table when you're Keto, what are you supposed to do? Make them as cups in the Instant Pot, sans carbs! It's quick and they are portable!

*Cook Time: 7 minutes // Servings: 4*

6 large eggs

2 strips of cooked bacon, sliced in ¼-inch (6-mm) wide pieces

½ cup (60 g) cheddar cheese, divided

¼ tsp sea salt

¼ tsp black pepper

1 cup (240 ml) water

1 tbsp (4 g) chopped fresh flat leaf parsley

In a small mixing bowl, beat the eggs. Add the cooked bacon, half of the cheese, sea salt and pepper, and mix well. Divide the egg mixture equally and pour it into four 4-ounce (114-g) ramekins and loosely cover with aluminum foil. Pour the water and place the trivet inside the inner pot. Place two ramekins on the trivet and stack the other two on the top.

Close the lid tightly and move the steam release handle to "Sealing." Turn the Instant Pot on by pressing the "Pressure Cooker/Manual" button. Set the timer for 7 minutes on HIGH pressure. When you hear the beeping sound indicating that the time has ended, carefully turn the steam release handle to the "Venting" position for the steam to escape and the float valve to drop down. Press "Cancel." Open the lid.

Top each ramekin with the remaining cheddar cheese, close the lid and melt the cheese for 2 minutes. Garnish with the chopped parsley and serve immediately.

*Nutrition:* Per Serving: 169 calories; 12g fat; 13g protein; 1g total carbohydrate; trace dietary fiber

# Slow-Cooked Granola On-the-Go

Most granola recipes contain oats or other grains, but this easy blend of nuts and seeds makes this recipe a great breakfast alternative when eaten with the milk of your choice. This dish is the only recipe in this book that uses the "Slow Cooker" function. You will not need the regular pressure cooker lid for this recipe, as the Instant Pot doesn't need to come to pressure.

*Cook Time: 2½ hours // Servings: 10*

1 cup (113 g) raw cashews

1 cup (173 g) raw almonds

1 cup (122 g) raw walnuts

1 cup (130 g) pumpkin seeds

1 tbsp (15 g) coconut oil

¼ cup (19 g) unsweetened coconut chips

1 tsp sea salt

1 tsp cinnamon (optional)

Dairy-free milk, for serving

In a large mixing bowl, combine all of the ingredients except for the coconut chips, sea salt and cinnamon, and mix well. Make sure all of the nuts are coated with the coconut oil.

Turn the Instant Pot on by pressing the "Slow Cooker" setting on "More." Place the nut mixture in the inner pot and cover the pot with a paper towel. Set the timer for 1 hour. When the timer goes off, stir the nuts. Set the timer for another hour.

Again, when the timer goes off, stir the nut mixture, making sure that the nuts are roasting evenly. Add the coconut chips. Set the timer for 30 minutes this time, or longer if more time is needed for all of the nuts to roast. The cashews should become a nice golden color.

When the timer goes off, spread out the nut mixture on a baking pan to cool and sprinkle with the sea salt and cinnamon. Serve with dairy-free milk or eat them plain as a snack. The mixture can be kept in an airtight container in a dry and dark place for up to 2 weeks.

---

*Nutrition:* Per Serving: 312 calories; 28g fat; 10g protein; 11g total carbohydrate; 4g dietary fiber

---

# Low-Carb Nutty Porridge

Porridge is a creamy and soothing breakfast that can start your day on the right track if you use the proper ingredients. This grain-free, low-carb porridge will keep you full for hours without sugar crash. Store the leftovers in an airtight container in the refrigerator for up to 1 week.

*Cook Time: 5 minutes // Servings: 4*

2½ cups (600 ml) water, divided

½ cup (57 g) blanched almond slivers

½ cup (56 g) raw cashews

¼ cup (32 g) raw pumpkin seeds

¼ head cauliflower, chopped

Pinches of sea salt, divided

¼ cup (60 ml) heavy whipping cream

¼ cup (60 g) hemp seeds, for topping

¼ cup (40 g) chia seeds, for topping

1 tbsp (7 g) cinnamon, for topping

1 tbsp (15 g) sweetener of your choice, optional, for topping

In a small bowl, add 2 cups (480 ml) of water, the almonds, cashews and pumpkin seeds. Soak for 30 minutes. Drain the water and set aside. Leave a few nuts and pumpkin seeds in a separate bowl to be used as garnish.

Turn the Instant Pot on by pressing the "Pressure Cooker/Manual" button and set the timer for 5 minutes on HIGH pressure. Pour the remaining ½ cup (120 ml) of water into the inner pot and then add the soaked nuts mixture, cauliflower and sea salt. Close the lid tightly and move the steam release handle to "Sealing." When the timer ends, you will hear a beeping sound. Allow the Instant Pot to cool down naturally until the float valve drops down and you can open the lid. Press "Cancel" and open the lid.

Transfer the cauliflower and nuts mixture to a blender, add the heavy cream and purée until smooth, similar to a creamy porridge consistency. If you prefer some texture, don't blend the nuts completely. Season with a pinch of sea salt. Garnish with the reserved nuts, pumpkin seeds, hemp seeds and chia seeds and serve immediately. Sprinkle with the cinnamon and the sweetener of your choice, if using.

*Nutrition:* Per Serving: 369 Calories; 30g fat; 15g protein; 16g total carbohydrate; 8g dietary fiber

# Eggs Three Ways: Hard-Boiled, Soft-Boiled and Poached

Making eggs is so easy in the Instant Pot. The eggs come out perfect every time and the eggshells peel so much easier than cooking them on the stovetop. Hard-boiled eggs make a wonderful protein-rich breakfast when you are in a hurry in the morning!

*Cooking Time: Poached Eggs – 2 minutes in a ramekin, Soft-Boiled Eggs – 4 minutes, Hard-Boiled Eggs – 6 minutes // Servings: 12*

**12 large eggs, at least 7 days old**

**1 cup (240 ml) water**

Turn on the Instant Pot by pressing the "Pressure Cooker/Manual" button and set the timer for the desired doneness of the eggs on HIGH pressure. Put 1 cup (240 ml) of water in the inner pot and place the trivet or a steamer basket inside. Gently place the eggs on the trivet or the steamer. Close the lid tightly and move the steam release handle to "Sealing." Place a large bowl in the sink and fill it with cold water. When you hear the beeping sound indicating that the time has ended, carefully turn the steam release handle to the "Venting" position to let the steam escape and the float valve drop down. Press "Cancel," and open the lid carefully.

Move the eggs into the bowl in the sink and peel the eggs. They should peel very easily. Store the peeled eggs in an airtight container in the refrigerator. It's best to eat hard-boiled eggs fresh, but they will be good for up to 3 days in the refrigerator. For poached eggs, it's best to put them in ramekins (see Eggs en Cocotte, page 18) and use a spoon to eat them since the whites will be still soft.

To reheat the peeled cold hard-boiled eggs, place them on the trivet with ½ cup (120 ml) of water in the inner pot for 2 minutes on HIGH pressure. Release the pressure manually when the timer ends and the eggs will be warm and as fresh as new.

*Nutrition:* Per Serving: 74 calories; 5g fat; 6g protein; trace total carbohydrate; 0g dietary fiber

> **Note:** To make peeling easier, it's best to use at least 7-day-old eggs. But to make peeling any eggs easier, crack the eggshells of all of the eggs as soon as you put them in the cold water so water can seep in between the membrane and the white part to cool down.

# Nourishing Soups and Stews

Soups are classic comfort foods in any culture. They're a nutritious way to satiate your appetite while feeding your body and soul. There is no other feeling that compares to sitting down for a big bowl of hot soup after a long day or when you are not feeling too well. And how can I talk about soups without mentioning nourishing Classic Bone Broth (page 30) and Various Stocks (page 33)? Home-cooked broth or stock adds rich flavor to any recipe you cook, so make batches in advance and freeze them to use in all your cooking.

Soups like the Heal Everything Chicken Soup (page 34) or Italian Seafood Soup (Cioppino) (page 45) are so simple to make in the Instant Pot that you'll be surprised why you used any other methods before. Korean Short Rib Soup with Radish (Gal Bi Tang) (page 42) is one of my family's favorites since it's meaty but still very refreshing because of the radish. Keto Zuppa Toscana (page 49) is a modified version of a carb-heavy soup from Tuscany, but it's filling and tasty just the same.

Meaty stews like the Best Keto Beef Stew (page 54), Chili con Carne (page 65) and even the Latin American Oxtail Stew (Sancocho) (page 58) will make even non-Keto family members forget about the carbs.

# Classic Bone Broth

Bone broth is rich in collagen and has good saturated fats. But it takes hours of simmering the bones in a pot on the stovetop and watching it to make sure it doesn't overflow. Not in the Instant Pot! Put the bones and water in, set the timer and forget about it until it's done! And what's even better is that nothing escapes and all the goodness is sealed right in during the cooking process. You will use this bone broth for many recipes that require broth or water for richer flavor and nutrients, both in this cookbook and beyond!

*Cook Time: 4 hours // Servings: 8*

**2–3 lbs (0.9–1.3 kg) bones, knuckles, long bones and marrow bones**

**8 cups (1.92 L) filtered cold water, or fill up to below the Max line**

Wash the bones in cold water and place them in the inner pot. Add enough cold water to immerse the bones completely. Soak the bones in the water for 30 minutes to an hour to let the blood out of the bones. When ready, drain the water and rinse until the water is clear. Place the bones back in the inner pot and fill the pot with 8 cups (1.92 L) of cold filtered water or up to below the Max line.

Close the lid tightly and move the steam release handle to "Sealing."

Turn the Instant Pot on by pressing the "Pressure Cooker/Manual" button. Set the timer for the maximum 120 minutes on HIGH pressure. If you have a newer model, choose the "Soup/Broth" function that has a preset time for up to 4 hours.

For older models, after the cooker beeps indicating that the time ended, hit "Cancel," and press the "Pressure Cooker/Manual" button and set the timer for another 120 minutes on HIGH pressure.

When the timer ends, allow the Instant Pot to cool down naturally until the float valve drops down. Press "Cancel" and open the lid. Since the pot is almost full of high-fat liquid, this make take up to 45 minutes.

At this time, the broth will be VERY rich. If you want the collagen to gel, you can store the broth in glass containers or jars and refrigerate. They will be good for up to a week. Or freeze in freezable Mason jars.

---

*Nutrition:* Per Serving: 176 calories; 11g fat; 17g protein; 0g total carbohydrate; 0g dietary fiber

---

**Note:** There is no right way to make bone broth. Using more knuckle bones will make the broth more gelatinous because of the cartilaginous parts from the soft tissues that surround the joints. Using long bones will give you more marrow. You can add vegetables and herbs or even roast the bones before making broth. But I also like to make plain versions to use as a base broth for various recipes, as you will see in this book.

# Various Stocks: Beef, Chicken, Fish, and Vegetable

The difference between stock and broth is that stock uses meaty parts with bones, vegetables and herbs, but bone broth is made with mainly bones. Stock is richer and commonly used to flavor foods. Making stock is quicker than making bone broth, but cooking it in a pressure cooker breaks the fibers down and creates deeper flavors. And you don't have to watch the pot on the stove! You will use the stock to flavor many recipes in this cookbook and the future!

*Cooking Time: 15-60 minutes // Servings: 6*

## VEGETABLE STOCK

1 large onion, quartered

1 carrot, cut in half

2 celery stalks, cut in half

2 dried whole bay leaves

1 bunch of fresh flat leaf parsley with stems

2 tbsp (17 g) peppercorns

3 sprigs of fresh thyme or 2 tsp (3 g) of dried thyme

1 head of garlic, crushed

5 cups (1.2 L) of water or fill up to below the Max line

## BEEF STOCK

2 lbs (900 g) inexpensive cut of meat, like beef shank bones or chuck roast

## CHICKEN STOCK

1 carcass of a whole chicken or 2 chicken legs—drumsticks, thighs and wings

## FISH STOCK

4 fish heads, tails and bones

1 lb (450 g) of any shellfish

To make the various stocks, start with the vegetable stock ingredients and add the meat ingredients for the different types of stock to the inner pot. In other words, to make the beef stock, combine the ingredients for the vegetable stock and the beef stock to the inner pot.

Close the lid tightly and move the steam release handle to "Sealing."

Press the "Pressure Cooker/Manual" button and set to the appropriate time depending on the stock you are making, on HIGH pressure.

**Vegetable Stock** – 15 minutes
**Beef Stock** – 60 minutes
**Chicken Stock** – 30 minutes
**Fish Stock** – 20 minutes

After the timer ends, allow the Instant Pot to cool down naturally until the float valve drops down. Press "Cancel" and open the lid. Refrigerate the stock in an air tight container for up to 2 weeks.

*Nutrition:* **Vegetable Stock:** Per Serving: 51 calories; trace fat; 2g protein; 12g total carbohydrate; 4g dietary fiber
**Beef Stock:** Per Serving: 262 calories; 14g fat; 14g protein; 12g total carbohydrate; 4g dietary fiber
**Chicken Stock:** Per Serving: 177 calories; 9g fat; 14g protein; 12g total carbohydrate; 4g dietary fiber
**Fish Stock:** Per Serving: 203 calories; 3g fat; 32g protein; 13g total carbohydrate; 4g dietary fiber

**Note:** As I mentioned in the bone broth recipe, you can make stock with "spent bones" from meals you've previously prepared. Freeze enough bones to make a full batch and follow these steps.

# Heal Everything Chicken Soup

One of the first recipes I made in the Instant Pot was this chicken soup. It's not only easy but it also tastes so much better with all the flavors that get sealed in while cooking. You don't have to watch over the stove or clean up a mess afterwards. This will be your go-to recipe when your family is under the weather for any reason. Make a double batch and freeze one for an emergency.

*Cooking Time: 30 minutes // Servings: 6*

1 medium onion, roughly sliced

3 medium cloves of garlic, crushed

2 medium carrots, roughly chopped

1 medium celery stalk, roughly chopped

1 medium parsnip, cut in 2-inch (5-cm) cubes

1 (3-lb [1.4-kg]) whole chicken, quartered

1 tbsp (15 g) sea salt

1 tbsp (7 g) fresh ground black pepper

¼ cup (15 g) fresh flat leaf parsley, reserve 1 tbsp (4 g) for garnish

1 tbsp (7 g) Italian seasoning

2 dried whole bay leaves

6 cups (1.44 L) cold filtered water or fill to below the Max line

In the inner pot, add the vegetables on the bottom first, then the chicken, sea salt, pepper and the herbs on top. Add the cold filtered water or fill up to below the Max line.

Close the lid tightly and move the steam release handle to "Sealing."

Turn on your Instant Pot by pressing the "Pressure Cooker/Manual" button. Set the timer for 30 minutes on HIGH pressure. After the timer ends, allow the Instant Pot to cool down naturally until the float valve drops down. Since the pot is almost full of high-fat soup, this might take up to 30 to 45 minutes.

Press "Cancel" and open the lid. Take out the chicken and debone the meat. Reserve the bones to make bone broth. Put the meat back in the pot and stir. Crush the carrots and celery gently against the side of the pot with the back of a spoon. Add more sea salt and black pepper, if needed, before serving. Garnish with the reserved fresh parsley and serve immediately.

*Nutrition:* Per Serving: 570 calories; 31g fat; 63g protein; 6g total carbohydrate; 1g dietary fiber

# Low-Carb New England Clam Chowder

One of the best vacations my family had was on a beach where we dug for clams every day. There is nothing that compares to eating freshly caught seafood, and fresh clams are no exception. We ate clams cooked in every way possible. They were all delicious, but this New England clam chowder was—and still is—my favorite way to eat clams. This comforting soup reminds me of the sea-salty ocean breeze as it warms my insides. The traditional version uses potatoes and flour as a thickener, but this low-carb version is lighter and even better than the conventional!

*Cook Time: 16 minutes // Servings: 8*

4 cups (960 ml) warm water

½ cup (122 g) kosher sea salt

2 lbs (900 g) live littleneck clams

2 cups (480 ml) cold water, reserve ½ cup (120 ml) for making slurry

2 tbsp (30 g) butter

1 cup (225 g) finely chopped bacon

1 medium onion, chopped

2 celery stalks, chopped

2 medium carrots, chopped

1 cup (133 g) parsnips, cut in 1-inch (2.5-cm) cubes

1 dried whole bay leaf

2 sprigs of fresh thyme

1 tsp dried tarragon

¼ cup (15 g) chopped fresh flat parsley, reserve 1 tbsp (4 g) for garnish

1 tbsp (8 g) tapioca flour

½ cup (120 ml) white wine

1 cup (240 ml) heavy whipping cream

Fill a glass roasting pan with the warm water and add the kosher sea salt. Stir to dissolve the sea salt. Place the clams in the pan and submerge them in a single layer. Let the clams de-sand for about 30 minutes. You will see water and sand spewing out of the clams so have towels ready to wipe down the counter.

After the clams are de-sanded, scrub the shells and clean them thoroughly. Discard the water.

Turn on the Instant Pot by pressing "Sauté" and set to "More." Add 1½ cups (360 ml) of cold water and the clams to the inner pot. Cover with a glass lid and cook for about 3 to 5 minutes until the clams open. Lift the clams out of the pot. Use a fork to pull the clams (and their juices) out of their shells into a large bowl and set aside. Discard the shells and any unopened clams. Carefully strain the clam juice in the inner pot through a metal strainer into the bowl with clams. Rinse the inner pot of any debris and shell pieces, dry the outside and put it back in the Instant Pot.

The Instant Pot setting should still be on "Sauté." Add the butter and bacon pieces to the inner pot and sauté for 4 minutes or until the bacon pieces are cooked. Add the clams, juices and remaining ingredients except for ½ cup (120 ml) of cold water, 1 tablespoon (4 g) of fresh parsley, the wine, heavy whipping cream and tapioca flour to the inner pot.

Close the lid tightly and move the steam release handle to "Sealing." Press the "Pressure Cooker/Manual" button and set the timer for 5 minutes on HIGH pressure. Meanwhile, whisk the tapioca and reserved ½ cup (120 ml) of water to make a slurry.

When the timer ends and you hear beeping sounds, carefully move the Steam Release Handle to "Opening," let the steam escape and wait until the float valve drops down. Press "Cancel" and open the lid carefully. Press "Sauté" and add the wine to the inner pot and stir. Add the heavy whipping cream and the tapioca mixture and mix for about 2 minutes until the soup thickens. Press "Cancel." Ladle the soup into 4 bowls, garnish with the reserved parsley and serve immediately.

*Nutrition:* Per Serving: 333 calories; 14g fat; 32g protein; 16g total carbohydrate; 2g dietary fiber

# Cream of Mushroom Soup

Cream of Mushroom Soup is my husband's favorite soup. It's subtle, yet so flavorful. No wonder there are so many recipes that call for a can of cream of mushroom soup as a base flavor. But I don't use the canned variety with additives and sugar. Instead, I make it in the Instant Pot. Besides the fact that I know exactly what's in the soup, it costs a lot less. You can either can or freeze this soup for future use in recipes or eat it right away, like my husband does!

*Cooking Time: 15 minutes // Servings: 6*

2 strips uncured bacon, chopped to ⅛-inch (3-mm) thickness

1 tbsp (15 g) butter

1 lb (450 g) white mushrooms, sliced

1 small onion, chopped

3 cloves garlic, chopped

2 cups (480 ml) chicken broth, reserve ½ cup (120 ml) for slurry

¼ tsp ground nutmeg

¼ tsp sea salt

¼ tsp black pepper

¼ cup (15 g) chopped fresh flat parsley with stem, plus 2 tbsp (8 g) leaves, for garnish

2 tbsp (16 g) tapioca flour

1 cup (240 ml) full-fat heavy cream

Turn on the Instant Pot by pressing "Sauté" and set to "More." Insert the inner pot and wait until the panel says "Hot." Add the bacon pieces and sauté for 5 minutes until crispy. With a slotted spoon, transfer the bacon bits to a small bowl. Leave about 1 tablespoon (15 ml) of bacon grease in the pot and transfer the rest to a heat-proof container to be used in your other recipes. Add the butter and the mushrooms to the inner pot and sauté for about 3 minutes or until soft and browned. Set aside a few pieces of the cooked mushrooms for garnish.

Add the onion, garlic, 1½ cup (360 ml) of the chicken broth, nutmeg, sea salt, black pepper and ¼ cup (15 g) of parsley. Stir to mix the ingredients.

Close the lid tightly and move the steam release handle to "Sealing." Press the "Pressure Cooker/Manual" button and set the timer for 5 minutes on HIGH pressure. Meanwhile, mix the tapioca flour, ½ cup (120 ml) of chicken broth and the heavy cream to make a slurry.

When the timer goes off, allow the Instant Pot to cool down naturally until the float valve drops down. Press "Cancel," and then, "Sauté." Open the lid, add the tapioca slurry to the inner pot and mix well while scraping the bottom of the pot for 1 minute or until the soup is thickened. Press "Cancel."

Transfer the soup into a blender and blend until smooth. Hot liquid can splatter suddenly while blending so be very careful. Pour the soup into 6 bowls and garnish with the reserved mushroom slices, bacon bits and parsley. Serve immediately.

*Nutrition:* Per Serving: 227 calories; 19g fat; 6g protein; 11g total carbohydrate; 2g dietary fiber

# Chicken Mulligatawny Soup

The name of this dish might be a bit tricky to pronounce, but once the silky creamy taste lingers in your mouth, you'll learn the name very quickly. There's something about the combination of coconut milk and spices that leaves your taste buds longing for more. Usually made with potatoes and lentils, this Indian soup is Keto-fied with cauliflower. I suggest taking the skin off the bone-in thighs, but if you need more fat, you can leave the skin on.

*Cooking Time: 18 minutes // Servings: 8*

4 tbsp (60 g) butter

1 small onion, chopped

1-inch (2.5-cm) piece fresh ginger, minced

1 celery stalk, chopped

2 small carrots, diced

2 tsp (4 g) curry powder

1 tsp sea salt

½ tsp freshly ground black pepper

⅛ tsp ground nutmeg

⅛ tsp dried thyme

8 chicken thighs, bone-in and skinless

3 cups (720 ml) chicken broth

2 cups (200 g) raw cauliflower rice or minced florets

2 cups (480 ml) full-fat coconut milk

¼ cup (4 g) chopped fresh cilantro plus 1 tbsp (1 g), for garnish

Turn on the Instant Pot by pressing "Sauté" and set to "More." Insert the inner pot and wait until the panel says "Hot." Melt the butter in the inner pot and sauté the onion and ginger for 2 minutes or until the onion is soft. Add the celery and carrots and stir for 1 minute. Add the remaining ingredients except for the coconut milk and cilantro. Hit "Cancel."

Close the lid tightly and move the steam release handle to "Sealing."

Press the "Pressure Cooker/Manual" button and set the timer for 15 minutes on HIGH pressure. When the timer ends, allow the Instant Pot to cool down naturally until the float valve drops down. Open the lid and stir in the coconut milk and cilantro. Press "Cancel." Ladle the soup into bowls and garnish with the reserved cilantro. Serve immediately.

*Nutrition:* Per Serving: 427 calories; 35g fat; 21g protein; 9g total carbohydrate; 3g dietary fiber

# Korean Short Rib Soup with Radish (Gal Bi Tang)

Traditionally, Korean Short Rib Soup (Gal Bi Tang) is one of the simplest, yet labor-intensive, Korean soups to make. It only has a few ingredients but takes a bit of preparation and hours of simmering on the stove that you must watch over. But not in the Instant Pot, because the bulk of the hard work is done without your constant attention. Not only that, the tender meats and the good fats make the broth that much more intense in flavor than if you were making it on the stove. If you love bone broth, you'll love this meaty soup for nourishment.

*Cooking Time: 55 minutes // Servings: 10*

3 lbs (1.4 kg) of grass-fed beef short ribs

1 large onion, sliced

6 cloves of garlic, crushed

2 tbsp (30 g) sea salt

1 tsp fresh ground black pepper

5 cups (1.2 L) cold filtered water or up to below the Max line

2 lbs (900 g) of large Korean radish or daikon, cut into 2-inch (5-cm) cubes

5 scallions, 4 sliced diagonally into 2-inch (5-cm) pieces, 1 chopped into ½-inch (13-mm) pieces, for garnish

Place the short ribs in the inner pot of the Instant Pot and fill with enough water to submerge the bones. Soak the bones in the water for 30 minutes at room temperature. Drain the water, add fresh water and repeat until the water runs clear. If the bones are not separated, this is a good time to separate each bone from the other bones and score the meat against the grain.

Add the short ribs, onion, garlic, sea salt, black pepper and 5 cups (1.2 L) of cold water to the inner pot. Close the lid tightly and move the steam release handle to "Sealing." Press the "Pressure Cooker/Manual" button and set the timer for 50 minutes on HIGH pressure. When the timer ends, allow the Instant Pot to cool down naturally until the float valve drops down. Since the pot is almost full with high-fat soup, this may take up to 45 minutes. Open the lid and add the radish and the long scallion pieces. Press "Pressure Cooker/Manual" and set the timer to 5 minutes. When you hear the beeping sound, allow the Instant Pot to cool down naturally until the float valve drops down. Press "Cancel" and open the lid.

Ladle the soup into bowls and garnish with the reserved chopped scallions. Serve immediately.

*Nutrition:* Per Serving: 555 calories; 49g fat; 21g protein; 6g total carbohydrate; 2g dietary fiber

**Note:** Grass-fed short ribs contain more omega-3 fatty acid than factory-raised meats. The fat is very nutritious, and this soup will be very flavorful because of the fat content. But if you want less fat, cool down the soup first, refrigerate it overnight and skim half the hardened fat from the top and reserve it for other uses.

# Italian Seafood Soup (Cioppino)

If you could bottle the sea-salty ocean air surrounding Italy, this soup would come very close to it. The combination of various fresh seafood in this quintessential Italian soup reminds me of the ocean. If you need a quick soup to warm your insides but also daydream about a seaside escape, make this soup in the Instant Pot while planning your next vacation.

*Cooking Time: 10 minutes // Servings: 8*

1 small onion, chopped

3 cloves garlic, crushed

4 anchovy fillets

1 carrot, sliced

2 stalks of celery, sliced

1 cup (180 g) diced tomatoes

2 tbsp (32 g) tomato paste

1 tsp (2 g) Italian seasoning

2 dried whole bay leaves

½ lb (227 g) shrimp with shells, deveined

6 littleneck clams, de-sanded and washed

1 lb (450 g) mussels, de-sanded and washed

½ lb (227 g) squid, sliced into ½-inch (13-mm) thick rings and tentacles

6 large scallops

½ lb (227 g) cod or other meaty fish cut in 2-inch (5-cm) chunks

½ cup (120 ml) white wine

1 cup (240 ml) fish stock

¼ cup (15 g) chopped fresh flat leaf parsley, reserve 1 tbsp (4 g) for garnish

1 tbsp (15 ml) extra-virgin olive oil (EVOO) to drizzle on top

Turn on the Instant Pot by pressing the "Pressure Cooker/Manual" button. Set the timer for 10 minutes on HIGH pressure. Insert the inner pot and add all the ingredients in the order listed, except for 1 tablespoon (4 g) of parsley and the EVOO.

Close the lid tightly and move the steam release handle to "Sealing."

When the timer ends, allow the Instant Pot to cool down naturally until the float valve drops down. Press "Cancel" and open the lid. Ladle the soup into bowls, garnish with the reserved parsley, drizzle with EVOO and serve immediately.

*Nutrition:* Per Serving: 283 calories; 6g fat; 39g protein; 12g total carbohydrate; 1g dietary fiber

Note: I do use a little bit of wine for cooking, since most of the calories are cooked off. Still, if you have issues with alcohol in cooking, you can leave it out completely.

# Broccoli and Leek Soup

No two vegetables go as well together in a soup than broccoli and leek. Leek adds mellow sweetness to the broccoli. But trust me when I say that this soup is uber healthy without the high carbs!

*Cooking Time: 7 minutes // Servings: 4*

¼ cup (35 g) raw cashew nuts

2 tbsp (30 g) butter

1 cup (90 g) sliced leek whites and tender greens

1 small onion, sliced

2 large cloves of garlic, crushed

2 cups (350 g) broccoli florets and sliced stems

2 cups (480 ml) chicken broth

2 sprigs (2-inch [5-cm]) fresh tarragon, leaves removed and stems discarded, or 2 tsp (2 g) of dried tarragon

Sea salt and pepper to taste

¼ cup (60 ml) full-fat heavy cream, for topping

2 tsp (2 g) chopped fresh chives, for garnish

Soak the raw cashews in cold water for 30 minutes. After they're soaked, drain the water and set the nuts aside. Discard the water.

Turn on the Instant Pot by pressing "Sauté" and set to "More." Insert the inner pot and wait until the panel says "Hot." Melt the butter and sauté the leek, onion and garlic for 3 minutes or until the leek is soft. Add the cashews, broccoli, chicken broth and tarragon to the inner pot.

Close the lid tightly and move the steam release handle to "Sealing." Hit "Cancel," and then press the "Pressure Cooker/Manual" button and set the timer for 4 minutes on HIGH pressure. When the timer ends, carefully turn the steam release handle to the "Venting" position for the steam to escape and the float valve to drop down. Press "Cancel" and open the lid. Using an immersion blender, purée the soup until smooth. Add sea salt and pepper to taste, drizzle with the heavy cream and garnish with the chives before serving.

*Nutrition:* Per Serving: 301 calories; 24g fat; 9g protein; 16g total carbohydrate; 3g dietary fiber

# Keto Zuppa Toscana

The original version of this soup can feed an army because it is rich and heavy with carbs. This Keto version uses cauliflower, mushrooms and parsnips, but it is still hearty, so grab a big spoon and call the neighbors, because the soup's on!

*Cooking Time: 17 minutes // Servings: 8*

3 tbsp (45 ml) extra-virgin olive oil (EVOO)

1 small onion, diced

5 cloves garlic, crushed

1 lb (450 g) ground Italian sausage

3 cups (720 ml) chicken broth

1 cup (163 g) crushed tomatoes

½ medium head cauliflower, cut into florets

3 parsnips (½ lb [227 g]), cut into 1-inch (2.5-cm) cubes

1 medium zucchini (½ lb [227 g]) cut into 1-inch (2.5-cm) cubes

½ lb (227 g) mushrooms, sliced

1 tsp sea salt

1 tsp black pepper

1 tsp Italian seasoning

½ lb (227 g) chopped fresh kale

1 cup (240 ml) full-fat heavy cream

¼ cup (46 g) Parmesan cheese, plus more if desired

¼ cup (15 g) chopped fresh flat leaf parsley, reserve 2 tbsp (8 g) for garnish

Turn on the Instant Pot by pressing "Sauté" and set to "More." Insert the inner pot and wait until the panel says "Hot."

Add the olive oil and sauté the onion and garlic for 2 minutes or until the onion is soft. Then, add the ground sausage and sauté for 2 minutes or until the meat pieces are separated and no longer pink. Add the rest of the ingredients except for the kale, heavy cream, cheese and 2 tablespoons (8 g) of parsley. Close the lid tightly and move the steam release handle to "Sealing."

Press the "Pressure Cooker/Manual" button and set the timer for 15 minutes on HIGH pressure. When the timer ends, allow the Instant Pot to cool down naturally until the float valve drops down. Open the lid and add the kale, heavy cream, Parmesan cheese and parsley, and stir. Press the "Pressure Cooker/Manual" button and set the timer for "0" minutes on HIGH pressure.

When you hear the beeping sound indicating the timer has ended, turn the steam release handle to the "Venting" position carefully for the steam to escape and the float valve to drop down. Press "Cancel" and open the lid. Ladle the soup into bowls and garnish with the parsley before serving. Add extra Parmesan cheese on top, if desired.

*Nutrition:* Per Serving: 447 calories; 36g fat; 16g protein; 18g total carbohydrate; 5g dietary fiber

# Vietnamese Beef "Noodle" Soup (Pho)

You can't talk about noodle soup without mentioning the classic Vietnamese dish pho (pronounced "fuh"). Its aromatic taste comes from dry-roasting some of the herbs and spices before adding the other ingredients to make the broth. Since you already made the Beef Stock (page 33) or Bone Broth (page 30), you are done with the hard part. Instead of using rice noodles as it's traditionally eaten, use zoodles and you won't miss the carbs.

*Cooking Time: 37 minutes // Servings: 6*

1 tsp of ground cinnamon

½ tsp of ground coriander

½ tsp coriander seeds

½ tsp whole cloves

1 whole star anise, crushed

1 medium onion, roughly chopped

1 (3-inch [7.5-cm]) piece ginger, peeled and chopped

1 tsp chili pepper flakes

4 cloves of garlic, roughly chopped

1 cup (16 g) roughly chopped fresh cilantro, reserve 1 tsp per bowl for topping

1 tbsp (15 ml) coconut aminos or tamari

1 tbsp (15 ml) fish sauce

5 cups (1.2 L) beef stock

4 cups (600 g) zoodles or spiralized zucchini

½ lb (227 g) cooked sirloin steak, thinly sliced, for topping

4 scallions, thinly sliced, for topping

1 cup (100 g) raw bean sprouts, for topping

2 jalapeños, sliced, for topping

6 lime wedges, for topping

Turn on the Instant Pot by pressing "Sauté" and set to "More." Insert the inner pot and wait until the panel says "Hot." In the inner pot, add the cinnamon, ground coriander, coriander seeds, cloves and star anise, and stir for about 5 minutes or until fragrant and smoky. Stir constantly so as not to burn the spices. Add the onion, ginger and chili pepper flakes and stir for 2 minutes. Add the garlic, cilantro, coconut aminos or tamari, fish sauce and beef stock, and stir. Close the lid tightly and move the steam release handle to "Sealing." Press "Cancel," then the "Pressure Cooker/Manual" button and set the timer for 30 minutes on HIGH pressure.

When the timer ends, allow the Instant Pot to cool down naturally until the float valve drops down. This can take up to 20 to 30 minutes since the pot is almost full. Press "Cancel" and open the lid. Place the zoodles in bowls. Strain the pho broth into the bowls. Top the bowls with sliced beef, scallions, 1 teaspoon of cilantro, bean sprouts, sliced jalapeños and a lime wedge before serving.

*Nutrition:* Per Serving: 145 calories; 6g fat; 13g protein; 11g total carbohydrate; 3g dietary fiber

# Szechuan Beef Soup

If you miss having noodles on the Keto diet, the trick is to eat a hearty soup with lots of protein and fat. And this hearty Szechuan-style Chinese soup will be so filling that you won't even miss the original carb-heavy version. Still miss slurping on noodles? Try it with zoodles to avoid spiking your sugar level.

*Cooking Time: 30 minutes // Servings: 6*

1 lb (450 g) chuck roast beef, cut into 2-inch (5-cm) pieces

2 tbsp (30 ml) dry white wine

2 tbsp (30 ml) coconut aminos or tamari

1½ tbsp (23 g) minced fresh ginger

1½ tbsp (14 g) minced garlic

1 tbsp (15 g) spicy chili flakes

2 whole star anise

1 (3-inch [7.5-cm]) stick cinnamon

1 tbsp (15 ml) rice vinegar

5 cups (1.2 L) beef stock or bone broth

4 baby bok choy, cut in half lengthwise, for topping

5 cups (750 g) raw zoodles or spiralized zucchini

3 chopped scallions, for topping

Season the beef with the wine and coconut aminos or tamari and marinate for 5 minutes. Turn on the Instant Pot by pressing the "Pressure Cooker/Manual" button and set the timer for 30 minutes on HIGH pressure. Insert the inner pot and place all the ingredients except bok choy, zoodles and scallions.

Close the lid tightly and move the steam release handle to "Sealing."

Meanwhile, place the zoodles in 6 bowls. When the timer goes off, allow the Instant Pot to cool down naturally until the float valve drops down. Press "Cancel" and open the lid. Add the bok choy and close the lid for 2 minutes. Ladle the soup over the raw zoodles and garnish with the chopped scallions. The hot broth should make the zoodles softer. Serve immediately.

---

*Nutrition:* Per Serving: 351 calories; 20g fat; 27g protein; 18g total carbohydrate; 7g dietary fiber

---

# Best Keto Beef Stew

If there is one dish that everyone can label as a "comfort" food, it's this hearty and satiating stew. But when you're trying to reduce carbs, you might think beef stew is off the menu and can't enjoy a bowl without guilt. Not true if you follow this recipe! And what's even better is cooking it in the Instant Pot so you don't have to watch and stir the pot for hours. This will be your go-to meal any day of the week!

*Cooking Time: 37 minutes // Servings: 6*

1 lb (450 g) chuck roast or stew meat, cut into 1-inch (2.5-cm) chunks

½ tsp sea salt

½ tsp black pepper

2 tbsp (16 g) tapioca flour, divided

1 tbsp (15 g) butter

1 small onion, roughly chopped

2 cloves garlic, roughly chopped

1 tbsp (16 g) tomato paste

½ cup (82 g) crushed tomatoes

1 tbsp (15 ml) Worcestershire sauce

1 small carrot, peeled and cut into 2-inch (5-cm) chunks

2 celery stalks, cut into 2-inch (5-cm) chunks

2 parsnips, cut into 2-inch (5-cm) chunks

1 cup (77 g) white mushrooms, quartered

½ cup (120 ml) dry red wine

1 cup (240 ml) beef stock

1 (3-inch [7.5-cm]) sprig fresh thyme (or ½ tsp dried thyme)

1 (2-inch [5-cm]) sprig fresh tarragon (or ½ tsp dried tarragon)

1 large dried whole bay leaf

1 tsp garlic powder

1 tsp onion powder

1 tsp sea salt (or more to taste)

1 tsp black pepper (or more to taste)

1 small handful of fresh flat leaf parsley, chopped, reserve 1 tbsp (4 g) for garnish

Coat the meat with the sea salt, pepper and 1 tablespoon (8 g) of tapioca flour. Toss gently and set aside. Turn on the Instant Pot by pressing "Sauté" and set to "More." Insert the inner pot and wait until the panel says "Hot." Brown the meat in small portions, not crowding the surface of the pot. When all of the sides are browned, take them out and add a new batch. Repeat this until all the meat is browned. This shouldn't take more than 15 minutes.

When all the meat is browned, add it back to the inner pot. Add the remaining ingredients except for 1 tablespoon (4 g) of parsley and the remaining tapioca flour. Close the lid tightly and move the steam release handle to the "Sealing" position. Press the "Pressure Cooker/Manual" button and set the timer for 20 minutes on HIGH pressure.

When you hear the beeping sound indicating that the time has ended, carefully turn the steam release handle to the "Venting" position for the steam to escape and the float valve to drop down. Press "Cancel," and open the lid carefully.

Remove about a cup (240 ml) of the broth from the pot to a bowl, add the remaining tapioca flour and whisk vigorously. Add the slurry back to the pot and stir gently. Press the "Pressure Cooker/Manual" button and set on "Less" to simmer and stir for 2 minutes or until the stew thickens. Press "Cancel," and ladle the stew into bowls, garnish with parsley and serve immediately.

*Nutrition:* Per Serving: 329 calories; 21g fat; 19g protein; 12g total carbohydrate; 2g dietary fiber

Note: If you like firmer vegetables in the beef stew, you can release the steam manually 15 minutes after the timer ends, add the vegetables and continue to cook for 5 more minutes until done and thickened.

# Low-Carb White Chili

For those who love chili but don't like tomatoes, white chili is a great alternative. This is a clean tasting yet hearty dish, like any other chili. Make batches of this Keto-friendly, low-carb chili and you can even have seconds without guilt!

*Cooking Time: 25 minutes // Servings: 6*

2 tbsp (30 g) butter

1 medium onion, chopped

3 cloves garlic, crushed

2 small stalks of celery, chopped

1 medium green bell pepper, cubed

2 lbs (900 g) ground turkey

½ tsp cumin

½ tsp cayenne pepper

2 cups (166 g) parsnips, cut into 1-inch (2.5-cm) cubes

1 cup (16 g) of chopped fresh cilantro, reserve ½ cup (8 g) for garnish

½ tsp chili pepper flakes

4 cups (960 ml) chicken broth

½ tsp sea salt (or more to taste)

½ tsp black pepper (or more to taste)

1 cup (122 g) shredded white cheddar cheese

½ cup (50 g) chopped fresh scallions, for garnish

Turn on the Instant Pot by pressing "Sauté" and set to "More." Insert the inner pot and wait until the panel says "Hot." Melt the butter in the inner pot and add the onion, garlic, celery and green pepper. Sauté for 3 minutes or until the onion and green pepper becomes a little soft. Add the ground turkey and sauté for 2 minutes or until the ground turkey is separated and no longer pink. Add the rest of the ingredients except for the cheese, ½ cup (8 g) of cilantro and the scallions. Stir to combine all of the ingredients.

Close the lid tightly and move the steam release handle to "Sealing."

Press "Cancel," then the "Pressure Cooker/Manual" button and set the timer for 20 minutes on HIGH pressure. When the timer ends, you will hear a beeping sound. Allow the Instant Pot to cool down naturally until the float valve drops down. Press "Cancel" and open the lid. Ladle the chili equally into 6 bowls, sprinkle with cheddar cheese and garnish with the rest of cilantro and scallions. Serve immediately.

*Nutrition:* Per Serving: 368 calories; 25g fat; 26g protein; 13g total carbohydrate; 3g dietary fiber

# Oxtail Stew (Sancocho)

*Sancocho* is a Latin American stew that's typically made with oxtail and starchy root vegetables, but this Keto version is much lighter while still rich in collagen and good fat. You can make this with chicken or short ribs, too!

*Cooking time: 60 minutes // Servings: 10*

2 lbs (900 g) oxtail bones

2 turnips, sliced into 1-inch (2.5-cm) pieces, divided in half

2 parsnips, sliced into 1-inch (2.5-cm) pieces, divided in half

1 small carrot, sliced into 1-inch (2.5-cm) pieces, divided in half

2 celery stalks, cut into 1-inch (2.5-cm) pieces, divided in half

½ green pepper, divided in half

4 cups (960 ml) cold water

4 cloves garlic, crushed

1 medium onion, sliced

1 tsp cumin

½ tsp turmeric

2 dried whole bay leaves

1 tsp sea salt

1 tsp black pepper

5 small tomatillos, roughly chopped

2 jalapeños, chopped

1 cup (16 g) chopped fresh cilantro, reserve ½ cup (8 g) for garnish

Wash and rinse the oxtail bones until the water runs clear. Place the oxtail bones, half of the turnips, parsnips, carrot, celery and green pepper in the inner pot. Add the water, garlic, onion, cumin, turmeric, bay leaves, sea salt and pepper to the inner pot.

Turn on the Instant Pot by pressing the "Pressure Cooker/Manual" button and set the timer for 30 minutes on HIGH pressure.

When you hear the beeping sound indicating that the time has ended, carefully turn the steam release handle to the "Venting" position for the steam to escape and the float valve to drop down. Press "Cancel," and open the lid carefully.

Add the remaining turnips, parsnips, carrot and celery, tomatillos, jalapeños and ½ cup (8 g) of the cilantro. Turn on the Instant Pot by pressing the "Pressure Cooker/Manual" button and set the timer for 30 minutes on HIGH pressure.

When the timer ends, you will hear a beeping sound. Allow the Instant Pot to cool down naturally until the float valve drops down. Press "Cancel" and open the lid. Ladle the stew into bowls, garnish with the remaining cilantro and serve immediately.

---

*Nutrition:* Per Serving: 684 calories; 65g fat; 9g protein; 15g total carbohydrate; 4g dietary fiber

---

**Note:** Half of the root vegetables are added in with the oxtails in the beginning to add flavor to the oxtail meat as it cooks. But those vegetables will be very soft when they are finished cooking. So, to add a little more texture, the remaining half is added at the end of the cooking. If you don't want to be bothered with adding them later, you can add all of them in the beginning with the oxtail bones, and set the timer to 60 minutes to release the pressure naturally.

# Spicy Korean Chicken Stew

If you love spicy foods, this stew is your dish. It's not as fatty as beef stew, but it's filling and oh-so-tasty. Of course, you can always adjust the amount of pepper so it's not too spicy.

*Cooking Time: 20 minutes // Servings: 6*

2 lbs (900 g) bone-in chicken thighs

⅓ cup (80 ml) coconut aminos or tamari

⅓ cup (80 ml) rice wine

¾ cup (180 ml) chicken stock

1 tsp sea salt

1 tsp black pepper

3 dried red chili peppers, or 2 tbsp (10 g) chili pepper flakes

2 tbsp (32 g) gochujang, or to taste

4 cloves of garlic, crushed

1 medium onion, sliced

1 green bell pepper, sliced

1 (1-inch [2.5-cm]) piece ginger, peeled and sliced

2 tsp (10 ml) sesame oil

3 scallions, cut into 2-inch (5-cm) pieces, reserve 1 tbsp (6 g) finely chopped for garnish

1 tsp toasted sesame seeds, for garnish

Turn on the Instant Pot by pressing the "Pressure Cooker/Manual" button and set the timer for 20 minutes on HIGH pressure.

Cut the excess skin and fat from the chicken thighs. Place the chicken thighs in the inner pot. Except for the chopped scallions and sesame seeds, combine the rest of the ingredients in a small mixing bowl and mix well. Taste to see if it needs more gochujang, chili peppers or sea salt to your taste. Add the sauce over the chicken in the Instant Pot and mix well. Pat down the chicken thighs so they are well coated with the sauce.

Close the lid tightly and move the steam release handle to "Sealing."

When the timer ends, allow the Instant Pot to cool down naturally until the float valve drops down. Press "Cancel," and open the lid.

Stir, ladle the chicken pieces in a shallow bowl, top with the chopped scallions, sprinkle on sesame seeds and serve immediately with Cauli Couscous (page 152).

*Nutrition:* Per Serving: 333 calories; 20g fat; 23g protein; 10g total carbohydrate; 1g dietary fiber

# Classic Italian Ratatouille

It's a wonderful discovery when the food you love—because it tastes so good—turns out to be so healthy for you that you can eat it every day without worrying about carbs. That's how I feel about ratatouille. It's so good that they even made an animated film about it. Okay, maybe that's stretching it a little, but this velvety stew is so good that I always need to make double batches in my house. I bet you will, too.

*Cooking Time: 5 minutes // Servings: 8*

¼ cup (60 ml) extra-virgin olive oil (EVOO)

1 medium onion, chopped

5 cloves garlic, crushed

½ cup (120 ml) chicken broth

2 tbsp (32 g) tomato paste

1 tsp dried thyme

1 tsp dried oregano

2 tsp (2 g) dried basil

½ cup (30 g) chopped fresh flat leaf parsley, reserve 1 tbsp (4 g) for garnish

2 tsp (10 g) sea salt

1 (½-lb [227-g]) eggplant, cut into 1-inch (2.5-cm) cubes

1 (1-lb [450-g]) zucchini, cut into 1-inch (2.5-cm) cubes

1 green bell pepper, chopped

4 tomatoes, chopped

¼ cup (60 ml) red wine

¾ cup (135 g) grated Parmesan cheese, reserve ¼ cup (45 g) for garnish

Zest from 1 unwaxed lemon, for garnish

Turn on the Instant Pot by pressing "Sauté" and set to "More." Insert the inner pot and wait until the panel says "Hot."

Add the EVOO to the inner pot. When the oil is hot, add the onion and garlic and sauté for 2 minutes or until the onion is soft. Add the remaining ingredients, except for 1 tablespoon (4 g) of parsley, the red wine, Parmesan cheese and lemon zest.

Close the lid tightly and move the steam release handle to "Sealing."

Press "Cancel," then, the "Pressure Cooker/Manual" button and set the timer for 1 minute on HIGH pressure. When you hear the beeping sound indicating that the time has ended, carefully turn the steam release handle to the "Venting" position for the steam to escape and the float valve to drop down. Press "Cancel," and then, "Sauté." Open the lid carefully. Add the red wine and Parmesan cheese. Stir and simmer for 2 minutes. Press "Cancel." Ladle into bowls, sprinkle the reserved parsley, Parmesan cheese and lemon zest, and serve immediately.

*Nutrition:* Per Serving: 244 calories; 13g fat; 20g protein; 13g total carbohydrate; 3g dietary fiber

# Chili con Carne

Chili was served during the cattle drives through Texas, as peppers and onions were cheap on the trail and beef was a bit expensive, so a side of beans was served for added protein. But then, the cowboys would mix the beans and chili together! At some point, beans were added to chili as one of the ingredients. But if you're a true chili connoisseur, skip the beans and make this Chili con Carne, since it's as original as it gets!

*Cooking Time: 17 minutes // Servings: 8*

1 guajillo pepper

1 cup (240 ml) warm water

2 tbsp (30 ml) extra-virgin olive oil (EVOO)

1 medium onion, chopped

6 garlic cloves, chopped

2 lbs (900 g) chuck roast, cubed

15 oz (430 g) crushed tomatoes

½ cup (120 ml) red wine

1 tbsp (7 g) cumin

2 tbsp (14 g) chili powder

1 tsp garlic powder

1 tsp dried oregano

½ cup (8 g) chopped fresh cilantro, reserve 1 tbsp (1 g) for garnish

½ cup (61 g) shredded cheddar cheese, for garnish

1 jalapeño pepper, sliced, for garnish

½ cup (60 g) sour cream, for garnish

To soften it, soak the guajillo pepper in the warm water.

Turn on the Instant Pot by pressing "Sauté" and set to "More." Insert the inner pot and wait until the panel says "Hot." Add the EVOO to the inner pot. When the oil is hot, add the onion and garlic and sauté for 2 minutes or until the onion is soft. Add one batch of the meat without crowding the pot and sauté to brown, about 2 minutes. You may need to sauté the meat in three batches. When all of the meat is browned, add the softened guajillo pepper and the rest of the ingredients except 1 tablespoon (1 g) of cilantro, the cheese, the jalapeño pepper and sour cream.

Close the lid tightly and move the steam release handle to "Sealing."

Press "Cancel," then the "Pressure Cooker/Manual" button and set the timer for 15 minutes on HIGH pressure. When the timer ends, you will hear a beeping sound. Allow the Instant Pot to cool down naturally until the float valve drops down. Press "Cancel" and open the lid. Ladle the chili into bowls, garnish with the reserved cilantro, cheddar cheese and jalapeño pepper slices. Add a spoonful of sour cream on top and serve immediately.

*Nutrition:* Per Serving: 475 calories; 34g fat; 30g protein; 12g total carbohydrate; 3g dietary fiber

**Note:** If guajillo pepper is not available, substitute 2 teaspoons (6 g) of cayenne pepper and add it to the rest of the ingredients for the browned meat mixture.

# Brazilian Fish Stew

This simple fish stew is quick to make and full of flavor. The recipe is for 6 servings but my husband could easily devour the whole thing by himself. Okay that might be a little bit of an exaggeration, but since it has hardly any carbs, it's one of his favorite seafood dishes. And he doesn't have to go to Brazil to enjoy it!

*Cooking Time: 7 minutes // Servings: 6*

4 tbsp (60 ml) extra-virgin olive oil (EVOO), divided

2 dried whole bay leaves

2 tsp (4 g) paprika

1 small onion, thinly sliced

2 cloves garlic, crushed

1 small green bell pepper, chopped

1½ cups (245 g) diced tomatoes

1 tsp sea salt

1 tsp freshly ground black pepper

¼ cup (4 g) chopped fresh cilantro, divided

1 cup (240 ml) fish stock or water

1½ lbs (690 g) meaty fish, like cod or striped bass, cut into 2-inch (5-cm) chunks

Turn on the Instant Pot by pressing "Sauté" and set to "More." Insert the inner pot and wait until the panel says "Hot." Add the EVOO and, when the oil is hot, add the bay leaves and paprika. Sauté for about 30 seconds or until the paprika is moist. Add the onion, garlic, bell pepper, tomatoes, sea salt, pepper and 2 tablespoons (2 g) of the cilantro.

Stir for 2 minutes until the onion is soft. Add the fish stock, then nestle the fish pieces among the vegetables in the pot. Close the lid tightly and move the steam release handle to "Sealing."

Press the "Pressure Cooker/Manual" button and set the timer for 5 minutes on HIGH pressure. When the time ends, you will hear a beeping sound, and then the "Warm" setting will start. At 5 minutes on "Warm," carefully turn the steam release handle to the "Venting" position for the steam to escape and the float valve to drop down. Press "Cancel," and open the lid carefully.

Divide the stew among bowls. Drizzle with the remaining 1 tablespoon (15 ml) of olive oil, sprinkle with the remaining 2 tablespoons (2 g) of cilantro and serve immediately.

---

*Nutrition:* Per Serving: 205 calories; 11g fat; 21g protein; 4g total carbohydrate; 1g dietary fiber

---

# Protein-Packed Grazers

The recipes in this chapter are designed to be served as the main course, packed with the most nutrients in a meal. I highly recommend grass-fed and pastured meats when on a Keto diet. Not only are most of the grass-fed and pastured animals humanely raised and slaughtered, their meats contain more nutrients than conventional meats.

These fat- and protein-rich recipes like Standing Herb-Crusted Prime Rib Roast (page 70), Affordable Osso Buco (page 73) and Texas-Style BBQ Baby Back Ribs (page 97) can be served with the vegetables of your choice or Nourishing Cauli Mash (page 164). But whatever you choose to serve with these high-fat and low-carb main dishes, the important thing is that you're eating foods that will satisfy your appetite and not spike your insulin.

# Standing Herb-Crusted Prime Rib Roast

When I first started using the Instant Pot, I didn't want to take a chance on cooking an expensive cut of meat like prime rib roast in the pot. But after years of using the appliance, I've perfected the unthinkable: I've achieved making the best prime rib roast in record time using the Instant Pot. If you want to make an intimate dinner for a special occasion, make this showstopper without breaking a sweat!

*Cooking time: 40 minutes // Servings: 6*

1 tbsp (15 g) sea salt

1 tbsp (7 g) black pepper

1 tbsp (7 g) garlic powder

1 tbsp (7 g) onion powder

1 tsp chopped fresh flat leaf parsley

1 tsp dried basil

1 tsp dried rosemary

1 tsp dried thyme

1 tsp dried tarragon

1 tsp mustard powder

1 (5–6 lb [2.2–2.7 kg]) two-bone prime rib roast, frenched (bones cut away from the meat cap and then tied together again with kitchen twine)

1 cup (240 g) water

1 cup (154 g) diced onion

2 tbsp (30 g) butter

---

*Nutrition:* Per Serving: 1186 calories; 99g fat; 64g protein; 5g total carbohydrate; 1g dietary fiber

---

In a small bowl, mix the spices and herbs. Place the prime rib roast on a cutting board and pat the meat dry with a paper towel or kitchen towel. Coat the surfaces with the herb mixture and leave about 1 tablespoon (7 g) of the herb mixture to coat again later. In the inner pot of the Instant Pot, add the water and diced onion. Place the rib roast bone side down. Cover tightly and refrigerate for 24 hours.

When ready to cook, take out the inner pot with the roast from the refrigerator and place it in the Instant Pot.

Turn on the Instant Pot by pressing the "Pressure Cooker/Manual" button and set the timer for 30 minutes on HIGH pressure. If your roast is smaller than 5 pounds (2.2 kg), set the timer for 25 minutes. Close the lid tightly and move the steam release handle to "Sealing."

Preheat the oven to 500°F (260°C) and prepare a roasting pan with a rack to sear the roast.

When the timer ends, you will hear a beeping sound. Allow the Instant Pot to cool down naturally until the float valve drops down, which should take about 10 minutes or less. If the valve does not drop down in 10 minutes after the timer ends, turn the steam release handle to the "Venting" position and allow the steam to release. When the valve drops down, open the lid. Press "Cancel," and take out the roast to the cutting board.

With a basting brush, cover the roast with butter and sprinkle the reserved herb mixture. Insert an ovenproof meat thermometer into the middle of the roast. Place the roast on the rack of the roasting pan and put the pan in the oven. Sear the roast until the internal temperature is 120°F (49°C) for rare and at 130°F (54°C) for medium rare.

Meanwhile, reserve the au jus from the inner pot in a bowl to serve with the roast later. You can make the Nourishing Cauli Mash (page 164) or Roasted Brussels Sprouts (page 102) while the roast is in the oven.

Once the roast is done to your liking, take it out to rest. While resting, the temperature of the meat should rise to 125°F (52°C) for rare or 135°F (57°C) for medium rare. Discard the kitchen twine, save the bones for making Beef Stock (page 33) or Classic Bone Broth (page 30) and slice the roast. Serve immediately with au jus from the inner pot and a side of fresh grated horseradish and Roasted Brussels Sprouts (page 102) or Nourishing Cauli Mash (page 164).

# Affordable Osso Buco

The first time I tried osso buco, I fell in love; I mean, with my meal. It was tender and so rich, braised with briny and smoky tomato sauce. Osso buco is usually made with veal shank bones, which are pricey, and it takes hours to make in a Dutch oven. So, I created this recipe with a cheaper cut, beef soup bones, which are basically the same cut from a cow. This version is just as tender and juicy. Serve with Nourishing Cauli Mash (page 164) and you won't miss the carbs!

*Cooking Time: 50 minutes // Servings: 4*

1 sprig fresh rosemary

1 sprig fresh thyme

1 dried whole bay leaf

2 whole cloves

3 (1–1½-lb [450 g–680-g]) whole soup bone shanks

1 tsp sea salt

1 tsp black pepper

¼ cup (60 ml) extra-virgin olive (EVOO), divided

1 small onion, diced into ½-inch (13-mm) cubes

3 cloves garlic, crushed

1 small carrot, diced into ½-inch (13-mm) cubes

1 stalk celery, diced into ½-inch (13-mm) cubes

2 tbsp (32 g) tomato paste

1 cup (240 ml) dry red wine

1 cup (240 ml) beef stock

2 tbsp (30 ml) Worcestershire sauce

3 tbsp (12 g) fresh flat leaf parsley, finely chopped, for garnish

1 tbsp (9 g) lemon zest

Place the rosemary, thyme, bay leaf and cloves into a cheesecloth and secure with kitchen twine. This will be the *bouquet garni*. Pat dry the soup bones with a paper towel to remove any excess moisture. Tie the meat to the bone with the kitchen twine. Season each shank with sea salt and black pepper.

Turn on the Instant Pot by pressing "Sauté" and set to "More." Insert the inner pot and wait until the panel says "Hot." Add 2 tablespoons (30 ml) of EVOO and when it's hot, brown all sides of the beef shanks, about 2 minutes per side. Remove the browned shanks and set aside.

Add the remaining EVOO to the inner pot and add the onion, garlic, carrot and celery. Sauté for 3 minutes or until the onion is soft and translucent. Add the tomato paste and mix well. Return the browned shanks to the inner pot, add the wine, the *bouquet garni*, beef stock and Worcestershire sauce. Stir to mix well and spoon the liquid over the beef shanks.

Close the lid tightly and move the steam release handle to "Sealing."

Press "Cancel," then the "Pressure Cooker/Manual" button and set the timer for 35 minutes on HIGH pressure. When the timer ends, you will hear a beeping sound. Allow the Instant Pot to cool down naturally until the float valve drops down. Press "Cancel," and then "Sauté." Open the lid and carefully remove the cooked shanks from the pot and put them on a serving platter. Remove and discard the *bouquet garni* from the pot. Simmer for about 5 minutes and reduce the sauce by half. Press "Cancel."

Remove the kitchen twine from the soup bones and discard. Pour the reduced sauce from the pot over the shanks. Garnish with the chopped parsley and lemon zest. Serve with a vegetable of your choice or with Nourishing Cauli Mash (page 164).

*Nutrition:* Per Serving: 929 calories; 51g fat; 92g protein; 8g total carbohydrate; 1g dietary fiber

# Easy Boeuf Bourguignon

If anyone knows Julia Child, he or she would also know that boeuf bourguignon was the signature dish on her cooking show. I can still hear her saying the name of this quintessential French dish with her English accent. It may be very difficult to master her technique, which makes people shy away from making it, but when you use the Instant Pot, it's a cinch. And with this Keto version, you'll want to make it every week.

*Cooking Time: 52 minutes // Servings: 8*

2 lbs (900 g) boneless sirloin steak, cut into 1-inch (2.5-cm) pieces

4 cups (960 ml) red wine, like Burgundy

1 tbsp (15 g) sea salt

½ tsp black pepper

6 tbsp (48 g) tapioca flour, reserve 2 tbsp (16 g) for slurry

4–6 strips uncured smoked bacon, chopped

3 tbsp (45 g) butter

1 medium onion, chopped

4 garlic cloves, chopped

2 small celery stalks, chopped

2 small carrots, cut into 1-inch (2.5-cm) chunks

1 lb (450 g) fresh mushrooms, quartered

1 dried whole bay leaf

1 tsp dried thyme

1½ cups (360 ml) beef stock, reserve 1 cup (240 ml) for slurry

1 tbsp (16 g) tomato paste

1 cup (125 g) frozen pearl onions

3 tbsp (45 ml) Worcestershire sauce

Sea salt and black pepper to taste

½ cup (30 g) chopped flat leaf parsley, for garnish

Dry the beef chunks well with a paper towel. Marinate the meat in the red wine, sea salt and pepper overnight.

The next day, strain the beef and reserve the wine. With a paper towel, dry the beef well and place it in a bowl. Coat all sides with the tapioca flour, sea salt and pepper and set aside.

Turn on the Instant Pot by pressing "Sauté" and set to "More." Insert the inner pot and wait until the panel says "Hot." Add the chopped bacon and the meat pieces to brown the meat. Don't crowd the meat and stir to brown all sides. This should take about 15 minutes. When all the batches are done, take them out and set them aside. Melt the butter and add the chopped onion, garlic, celery and carrots and sauté for 3 minutes or until the onion is soft. Add the reserved wine and scrape the sides and the bottom of the pot. Let the wine bubble for about 2 minutes. Add the meat back into the pot with the mushrooms, bay leaf, thyme, ½ cup (120 ml) of beef stock and tomato paste, and stir.

Press "Cancel," then close the lid tightly and move the steam release handle to "Sealing." Then, press the "Pressure Cooker/Manual" button and set the timer for 30 minutes on HIGH pressure.

Meanwhile, combine the remaining tapioca flour with the remaining beef stock.

When the timer ends, you will hear a beeping sound. Allow the Instant Pot to cool down naturally until the float valve drops down. Press "Cancel," then press "Sauté." Open the lid. Add the tapioca mixture and stir. Add the pearl onions and Worcestershire sauce. Sprinkle sea salt and pepper to taste. Stir to thicken the sauce for about 2 minutes. Press "Cancel." Transfer to shallow bowls, garnish with the parsley and serve immediately.

*Nutrition:* Per Serving: 502 calories; 23g fat; 34g protein; 17g total carbohydrate; 2g dietary fiber

# Pernil with Dirty Rice

I grew up working at my family's business in a diverse neighborhood in New York City with all kinds of ethnic foods. Pernil with *arroz con frijoles* was one of my favorite dishes for lunch. After I got married, I learned to cook pernil in the oven but rarely cooked it since it took so long. But since I started making it in the Instant Pot for a fraction of the time, I started making it more often. Even my kids, who have never been to the neighborhood where I worked, love it!

*Cooking Time: 48 minutes // Servings: 6*

2 strips of uncured bacon, finely chopped

1 tbsp (7 g) dried oregano

1 tbsp (7 g) cumin

1 tsp garlic powder

1 tsp onion powder

1 tsp paprika

1 tsp sea salt

1 tsp black pepper

1 tbsp (15 ml) apple cider vinegar (ACV)

1 tbsp (15 ml) extra-virgin olive oil (EVOO)

1 (4-lb [1.8-kg]) pork shoulder with skin

1 large onion, sliced

6 cloves garlic, crushed

½ cup (120 ml) chicken broth

½ cup (8 g) chopped fresh cilantro, divided

Juice from ½ of a lime plus 2 tbsp (30 ml) lime juice, divided

4 cups (400 g) Cilantro Lime Cauli Couscous (page 152)

Turn on the Instant Pot by pressing "Sauté" and set to "More." Insert the inner pot and wait until the panel says "Hot." Add the bacon pieces and sauté for 3 minutes or until crispy. With a slotted spoon, take out the bacon and leave the bacon grease inside. Press "Cancel" to turn off the Instant Pot.

In a small bowl, combine the oregano, cumin, garlic powder, onion powder, paprika, sea salt, black pepper, ACV and EVOO. Coat the pork shoulder with the herb mixture. Make sure to cover the meaty part first and use the rest on top of the skin. Place the sliced onion, garlic, chicken broth and ¼ cup (4 g) of cilantro in the inner pot and place the pork shoulder on top. Cover the inner pot tightly and refrigerate for at least 3 hours. When ready to cook, take the inner pot out of the refrigerator and squeeze the juice from ½ of a lime on top.

Turn on the Instant Pot by pressing the "Pressure Cooker/Manual" button and set the timer for 45 minutes on HIGH pressure. Place the inner pot with the marinated pork shoulder inside the cooker, close the lid tightly and move the steam release handle to "Sealing." Meanwhile, mix the cooked bacon with the Cilantro Lime Cauli Couscous to make the dirty rice.

When the timer ends, you will hear a beeping sound. Allow the Instant Pot to cool down naturally until the float valve drops down. Press "Cancel" and open the lid. Take out the pork, plate the meat and pour some of the cooking liquid on top. Garnish with the remaining cilantro and lime juice. Serve immediately with dirty rice.

---

*Nutrition:* Per Serving: 624 calories; 45g fat; 43g protein; 12g total carbohydrate; 4g dietary fiber

---

Note: An extra inner pot is handy when making multiple dishes. While the pork shoulder is marinating in one inner pot, you can make the Cilantro Lime Cauli Couscous in another inner pot. Or if you don't have two inner pots, you can marinate the pork shoulder in another container, so you can use the inner pot to make the dirty rice.

# Wonton Bites with Ginger Glaze

If you ask me, the best part about wontons is not the dough but the meat stuffing. So why bother spending time making wontons when what you really want is the inside? This recipe is quick to mix and steam in the Instant Pot, and you don't have to bother with wrapping them. Or you can serve on lettuce boats or steamed cabbage boats if you want to be fancy. The simple ginger umami glaze can be made in advance or quickly made in the Instant Pot after making the wontons.

*Cooking Time: 15 minutes // Servings: 5*

1 lb (450 g) ground pork

1 tsp grated ginger

2 cloves garlic, minced or pressed

½ tsp white pepper

2 tsp (10 ml) coconut aminos

2 tbsp (16 g) tapioca flour

¼ cup (13 g) finely chopped fresh chives or scallions, reserve 1 tbsp (3 g) for garnish

¼ cup (4 g) finely chopped fresh cilantro, reserve 1 tbsp (1 g) for garnish

1 cup (240 g) water

### GINGER GLAZE

1 tbsp (7 g) grated fresh ginger

½ cup (120 ml) coconut aminos

2 tbsp (30 ml) cold water

½ tsp tapioca flour

½ tsp sea salt

½ toasted sesame seeds

Combine all of the ingredients except for 1 tablespoon (3 g) of scallions and the cilantro for garnish in a medium-sized mixing bowl and mix well. Take about 1 to 2 tablespoons (15 to 30 g) of the mixture and make small bite-size balls.

Turn on the Instant Pot by pressing the "Pressure Cooker/Manual" button and set the timer for 15 minutes on HIGH pressure. Pour in the water and place a steamer basket—NOT the trivet that came with the Instant Pot—inside the inner pot. Place the wonton balls on the steamer basket in a single layer. Close the lid tightly and move the steam release handle to "Sealing." When the timer ends, you will hear a beeping sound. Allow the Instant Pot to cool down naturally until the float valve drops down. Press "Cancel" and open the lid. Transfer the wonton bites to a platter. Empty out the water inside the inner pot and make the Ginger Glaze by combining all the ingredients in a small saucepan and simmering on low heat for 2 minutes, or until the sauce thickens.

You can also make the ginger glaze in a small saucepan on the stove while the wontons are in the Instant Pot. Serve the wonton bites with the Ginger Glaze and garnish with the remaining scallions and cilantro.

*Nutrition:* Per Serving: 160 calories; 8g fat; 6g protein; 12g total carbohydrate; trace dietary fiber

**Note:** I like to use a little bit of tapioca flour to thicken sauces and gravy. For some people, this may cause a spike in glucose levels so avoid using it if this is a problem for you. But if tapioca flour does not cause problems for you, it's a better thickener than grain flours.

# Korean-Style Braised Short Ribs (Galbi Jjim)

This is my family's favorite Korean dish. The original recipe uses sugar but this Keto version uses kiwi, which also tenderizes the meat. This makes a large batch to save for several meals. You could easily halve the recipe for a smaller batch.

*Cooking Times: 50 minutes // Servings: 8*

4 lbs (1.8 kg) beef short ribs

5 cups (1.2 L) cold water

1 cup (240 ml) unsalted bone broth

½ cup (120 ml) rice wine or white wine

½ cup (120 ml) Bragg's coconut aminos or tamari

1 tsp sesame oil

1 medium onion, roughly sliced

6 large cloves of garlic, crushed

1 (1-inch [2.5-cm]) piece fresh ginger, peeled and finely chopped

1 carrot, roughly sliced into chunks

1 cup (116 g) radish or daikon, into 2-inch (5-cm) chunks

4 scallions, 3 cut into 1-inch (2.5-cm) pieces and 1 finely chopped, for garnish

1 cup (143 g) raw peeled chestnuts (optional)

1 tbsp (10 g) toasted sesame seeds, for garnish

Place the ribs on a cutting board, and cut and separate each bone with the attached meat. Score the meat against the grain and be careful not to cut it off the bones. In the inner pot of the Instant Pot, place the ribs and cover with 5 cups (1.2 L) of cold water and let them soak for about 30 minutes. Drain the water and repeat until the water is no longer pink. Strain the ribs and discard the water. Place the ribs in the inner pot and prepare the seasoning.

In a small mixing bowl, combine the bone broth, rice wine, coconut aminos and sesame oil. Pour the sauce over the ribs in the inner pot. Add the onion, garlic, ginger, carrot, radish, 1-inch (2.5-cm) scallion pieces and chestnuts, if using, on top of the ribs. Mix the ingredients to incorporate them.

Turn on the Instant Pot by pressing the "Pressure Cooker/Manual" button and set the timer for 50 minutes on HIGH pressure. Close the lid tightly and move the steam release handle to "Sealing." When the timer ends, you will hear a beeping sound. Allow the Instant Pot to cool down naturally until the float valve drops down. Press "Cancel" and open the lid. Plate the ribs and garnish with the sesame seeds and finely chopped scallion. Serve with Cauli Couscous (page 152).

*Nutrition:* Per Serving: 1111 calories; 96g fat; 50g protein; 10g total carbohydrate; 1g dietary fiber

# Liver Meatballs Marinara with Zoodles

Organ meats are so nutritious, but if your family is like mine, it's hard to get liver into their diet. What's a creative cook to do? Incorporate them into meatballs with their favorite sauce! Your family won't even know there's liver in these soft and tender meat/liver balls!

*Cooking Time: 22 minutes // Servings: 8*

2 strips uncured bacon, finely diced

1 lb (450 g) grass-fed cow liver

1 lb (450 g) ground beef

1 cup (154 g) diced onion, reserve ½ cup (77 g) for sauce

2 tbsp (19 g) finely minced garlic, reserve 1 tbsp (9 g) for sauce

2 tbsp (8 g) chopped fresh flat leaf parsley

¼ cup (10 g) chopped fresh basil, divided

1 tsp dried oregano

1 large egg, beaten

1 tsp sea salt

2 tbsp (30 g) butter

4 cups (968 g) crushed tomatoes

1 tsp Italian seasoning

3 zucchinis, spiralized to make zoodles

Sea salt and black pepper to taste

½ cup (91 g) grated Parmesan cheese

Turn on the Instant Pot by pressing "Sauté" and set to "More." Insert the inner pot and wait until the panel says "Hot." Add the bacon and sauté for 2 minutes or until the bacon is no longer pink. With a slotted spoon, take out the bacon pieces and place them into a large mixing bowl. Do not clean the pot. Press "Cancel."

Place the liver on the cutting board and cut out the blood vessels and hard nodules and discard. Put the liver in a food processor and purée. Transfer the liver purée into the large mixing bowl with the bacon. Add the ground beef, ½ cup (77 g) of diced onion, garlic, parsley, 2 tablespoons (5 g) of basil, oregano, egg and sea salt to the mixing bowl with the liver. Mix well and form 1- to 1½-inch (2.5- to 3.75-cm) meatballs and set them on a platter.

Press "Sauté" and set to "More." When the panel says, "Hot," melt the butter in the pot. In small batches, brown the meatballs until all of them are done. This shouldn't take more 10 minutes. Add the remaining garlic, onion, crushed tomatoes and Italian seasoning to the inner pot. Add the meatballs back into the pot and cover them with the sauce. Close the lid tightly and move the steam release handle to "Sealing."

Press "Cancel," then the "Pressure Cooker/Manual" button and set the timer for 10 minutes on HIGH pressure. When the timer ends, you will hear a beeping sound. Allow the Instant Pot to cool down for 10 minutes, then carefully turn the steam release handle to the "Venting" position for the steam to escape and the float valve to drop down. Press "Cancel." Open the lid carefully and stir the sauce to mix with the meatballs. Add the zoodles on top, do not mix. Close the lid and wait for 2 minutes. Plate the zoodles on a shallow bowl, place the meatballs on top and ladle the sauce over the meatballs. Sprinkle with the Parmesan cheese and garnish with the remaining basil. Serve immediately.

*Nutrition:* Per Serving: 400 calories; 20g fat; 38g protein; 18g total carbohydrate; 3g dietary fiber

# Smothered Pork Chops

Who loves making pork chops? Better yet, who loves *cleaning* after making pork chops? Not me. But these saucy pork chops made right in the Instant Pot will make you wonder why you ever made pork chops the old-fashioned way! You won't mind making these tender, fall-off-the-bone chops again and again, since there's no mess to clean up afterward!

*Cooking Time: 33 minutes // Servings: 4*

½ tsp garlic powder

½ tsp onion powder

1 tsp paprika

1 tsp sea salt

½ tsp black pepper

4 (6-oz [170-g]) boneless pork loin chops

2 strips of uncured bacon, finely chopped

1 tbsp (15 g) butter, more as needed

½ medium onion, sliced

12 oz (340 g) white mushrooms, sliced ¼-inch (6-mm) thick

½ cup (120 ml) white wine

½ cup (120 ml) full-fat heavy cream

1 tsp dried thyme

1 tsp dried tarragon

1 tbsp (15 ml) Worcestershire sauce

1 tbsp (8 g) tapioca flour, more if needed

¼ cup (15 g) fresh flat leaf parsley, chopped, reserve 1 tbsp (4 g) for garnish

In a small bowl, mix the garlic powder, onion powder, paprika, sea salt and black pepper. Sprinkle both sides of the pork chops with the garlic powder mixture and set aside.

Turn on the Instant Pot by pressing "Sauté" and set to "More." Insert the inner pot and wait until the panel says "Hot." Add the bacon and sauté for 3 minutes, then add the pork chops, two at a time, and brown both sides for 2 minutes per side. Add butter at this point if needed. Transfer the pork chops to a plate and set aside. Add the onion and mushrooms and sauté until the onion is soft. Add the white wine and stir and scrape the bottom for 1 minute. Place the pork chops on top of the onion and mushrooms.

Close the lid tightly and move the steam release handle to "Sealing." Press "Cancel," then the "Pressure Cooker/Manual" button and set the timer for 20 minutes on HIGH pressure. When the timer ends, you will hear a beeping sound. Allow the Instant Pot to cool down naturally until the float valve drops down. Press "Cancel" and open the lid. Place the pork chops on plates to be served and let rest. Meanwhile, add the rest of the ingredients in the inner pot except 1 tablespoon (4 g) of parsley and stir for 2 minutes or until it thickens. Add more tapioca flour if needed, depending on how much liquid was produced from the meat and vegetables from cooking. Top the pork chops with the mushroom gravy and garnish with parsley before serving.

*Nutrition:* Per Serving: 343 calories; 21g fat; 23g protein; 12g total carbohydrate; 2g dietary fiber

# Brisket with Cauli Mash

When I was growing up, I lived in a predominantly Jewish neighborhood in Queens. Brisket was always on the special holiday dinner menu and I was lucky enough to be invited to many of those dinners as the only gentile. This special Jewish dish is always a showstopper, but it takes hours to prepare. So, this recipe is my tribute to many of my friends' mothers who slaved over the stove to make this special dish every holiday. I think they'd be proud of my gentile method.

*Cooking Time: 68 minutes // Servings: 8*

4 lbs (1.8 kg) beef brisket

1 tsp sea salt

1 tsp black pepper

2 tbsp (30 ml) avocado oil

1 large onion, sliced

6 cloves garlic crushed

2 large carrots, sliced to 1-inch (2.5-cm) thickness

1 cup (240 ml) red wine

½ cup (120 ml) beef stock

2 tbsp (32 g) tomato paste

1 tbsp (15 ml) Worcestershire sauce

¼ cup (15 g) flat leaf parsley, chopped, 1 tbsp (4 g) reserved for garnish

2 sprigs of rosemary

1 tsp tapioca flour (optional)

Season the brisket well with sea salt and black pepper and set aside. Turn on the Instant Pot by pressing "Sauté" and set to "More." Insert the inner pot and wait until the panel says "Hot." Add the avocado oil to the inner pot. Add the brisket and brown the brisket well on both sides, about 5 minutes each side.

Remove the brisket and set aside. Add the onion and garlic and sauté for 3 minutes, or until the onion is soft. Add the rest of the ingredients except for the 1 tablespoon (4 g) of reserved parsley and simmer for 1 minute. Add the brisket back into the pot and spoon some of the vegetables on top.

Close the lid tightly and move the steam release handle to "Sealing."

Press "Cancel," then the "Pressure Cooker/Manual" button and set the timer for 50 minutes on HIGH pressure. When the timer ends, you will hear a beeping sound. Allow the Instant Pot to cool down naturally until the float valve drops down. Press "Cancel" and open the lid. Remove the brisket and let it rest for 10 minutes on a cutting board. Meanwhile, press "Sauté" on "LOW" and simmer the sauce for 5 minutes or until the sauce is reduced in half. If you'd like a thicker sauce, like a gravy, add the tapioca flour and stir for 2 to 3 minutes until it thickens. Press "Cancel," and open the lid. Slice the brisket against the grain, plate the beef slices, pour sauce/gravy over the meat, garnish with the remaining parsley and serve immediately with Nourishing Cauli Mash (page 164).

*Nutrition*: Per Serving: 790 calories; 64g fat; 39g protein; 7g total carbohydrate; 2g dietary fiber

# Low-Carb Beef Stroganoff

I remember reheating a frozen beef stroganoff TV dinner after school and wondering why anyone would eat such bad-tasting meat. Little did I know, it was the "frozen dinner" part that was bad, not beef stroganoff as a dish. This Keto-fied version is even better than regular homemade stroganoff and it will knock your socks off. I never thought I'd enjoy sour cream with meat as much as I do now!

*Cooking Time: 15 minutes // Servings: 4*

2 tbsp (30 g) butter

½ cup (77 g) diced onion

2 cloves garlic

1 lb (450 g) sirloin steak, cut into ½-inch (13-mm) thick and 2-inch x 1-inch (5 x 2.5-cm) strips

2 cups (10 oz [284 g]) white mushrooms, sliced

½ tsp garlic powder

½ tsp onion powder

½ cup (120 ml) beef stock

2 tbsp (30 ml) Worcestershire sauce

½ tsp sea salt

½ tsp black pepper

1 tbsp (8 g) tapioca flour

⅓ cup (40 g) full-fat sour cream

4 cups (720 g) raw zoodles or spiralized zucchinis

1 tbsp (4 g) fresh flat leaf parsley, chopped

Turn on the Instant Pot by pressing "Sauté" and set to "More." Insert the inner pot and wait until the panel says "Hot." Add the butter and sauté the onion and garlic for 2 minutes or until the onion is soft. Add the steak pieces in small batches and quickly sauté for 2 minutes or until the meat is no longer pink. Finish browning all of the meat, add the rest of the ingredients except for the tapioca flour, sour cream, zoodles and parsley into the inner pot.

Close the lid tightly and move the steam release handle to "Sealing." Press "Cancel," then the "Pressure Cooker/Manual" button and set the timer for 10 minutes on HIGH pressure.

When the timer ends, you will hear a beeping sound. Allow the Instant Pot to cool down naturally until the float valve drops down. Press "Cancel" and open the lid. Take out about half of the liquid to a bowl and mix with tapioca flour. Press "Sauté." Add the tapioca mixture and sour cream back in the pot and stir for 2 minutes until the gravy thickens. Add the zoodles on top and close the lid for 2 minutes. Spoon out the zoodles, pour the beef with mushroom gravy on top, garnish with the parsley and serve immediately.

*Nutrition:* Per Serving: 438 calories; 32g fat (66.4% calories from fat); 24g protein; 12g total carbohydrate; 1g dietary fiber; 95mg cholesterol; 704mg sodium

# Perfect Pot Roast

A pot roast can be an all-afternoon cooking affair in the oven. And you'd have to monitor the doneness until it's "fall-off-the-bone" tender. But in these busy times, have you got time for that? The Instant Pot makes this all-American dish a breeze to make and you don't have to babysit it! Turn it on and go make your favorite side dish without worries.

*Cooking Time: 94 minutes // Servings: 6*

3–4 lbs (1.4–1.8 kg) chuck roast

1 tbsp (15 g) sea salt

1 tbsp (6 g) fresh ground black pepper

2 tbsp (30 g) butter

1 large onion, sliced

4 cloves garlic, crushed

2 carrots, cut diagonally about
1 inch (2.5 cm) in length

2 celery stalks, cut diagonally about
2 inch (5 cm) in length

2 long daikon or turnip or radish,
cut into 2-inch (5-cm) large chunks

1 cup (240 ml) red wine

2 sprigs of fresh thyme

2 dried whole bay leaves

¼ cup (15 g) chopped flat leaf fresh
parsley with stems, reserve 1 tsp for
garnish

2 sprigs of fresh tarragon

1 tbsp (15 ml) Worcestershire sauce

¾ cup (180 ml) beef stock

Pat dry the meat, rub the sea salt and pepper on the outside and set aside.

Turn on the Instant Pot by pressing "Sauté" and set to "More." Insert the inner pot and wait until the panel says "Hot." Melt the butter and add the onion and garlic. Sauté for 2 minutes or until the onion is soft. Add the carrots and sauté for 2 minutes. Add the rest of the ingredients and stir around to mix. Place the chuck roast on top of the vegetables. Press "Cancel," and then press the "Pressure Cooker/Manual" button and set the timer for 90 minutes on HIGH pressure. Close the lid tightly and move the steam release handle to "Sealing."

When the timer ends, you will hear a beeping sound. Allow the Instant Pot to cool down naturally until the float valve drops down. Press "Cancel" and open the lid.

Take out the roast and allow it to rest for 5 minutes. Slice the beef, top it with the cooked vegetables, sauce and garnish with parsley before serving.

*Nutrition:* Per Serving: 646 calories; 39g fat; 58g protein; 11g total carbohydrate; 3g dietary fiber

# Keto Corned Beef and Cabbage

I don't know why we don't make corned beef and cabbage more often. We always make it in March, even though we're not Irish, and we enjoy it immensely. And now that I use the Instant Pot, I enjoy cooking it even more. But don't be like me and wait until March. This makes a great meal any day of the week, any month of the year!

*Cooking Time: 85 minutes // Serving: 6*

1 large onion, sliced

6 cloves garlic, crushed

1 pickling spice packet

5 cups (1.2 L) cold water

4 lbs (1.8 kg) corned beef brisket

2 dried whole bay leaves

1 head green cabbage

¼ cup (15 g) fresh flat leaf parsley, chopped, for garnish

Deli mustard, for serving

Turn on the Instant Pot by pressing the "Pressure Cooker/Manual" button and set the timer for 80 minutes on HIGH pressure.

In the inner pot, place the onion, garlic, pickling spices and water. Place the corned beef brisket, fat side up, and 2 bay leaves in the inner pot. Close the lid tightly and move the steam release handle to "Sealing."

When the timer ends, you will hear a beeping sound. Allow the Instant Pot to cool down naturally. If in 30 minutes, the float valve does not drop down, carefully turn the steam release handle to "Venting" and release the pressure. Open the lid, remove the corned beef and place it on a cutting board with a little bit of the liquid. Cover and let it rest.

Cut the cabbage into quarters and add it to the inner pot. Close the lid tightly, move the steam release handle to "Sealing," press "Cancel," and then the "Pressure Cooker/Manual" button and set the timer for 5 minutes on HIGH pressure.

When you hear the beeping sound indicating that the time has ended, carefully turn the steam release handle to the "Venting" position for the steam to escape and the float valve to drop down. Press "Cancel," open the lid carefully and move the cabbage onto a platter. Slice the corned beef against the grain and serve with the cabbage and parsley. Spoon a little bit of the reserved cooking liquid over the corned beef and cabbage and serve with deli mustard on the side.

*Nutrition:* Per Serving: 650 calories; 45g fat; 47g protein; 12g total carbohydrate; 4g dietary fiber

# Not Your Mama's Meatloaf

Everyone's favorite all-American dish is a cinch in the Instant Pot since it only takes 30 minutes to make. Serve with smooth and creamy Nourishing Cauli Mash (page 164) and you won't miss the carbs. Make an extra batch for an easy and healthy lunch the next day!

*Cooking Time: 30 minutes // Servings: 8*

½ lb (227 g) ground sirloin beef

½ lb (227 g) ground pork

2 large eggs, beaten

¼ cup (38 g) finely chopped onion

1 clove garlic, minced

½ cup (49 g) extra fine blanched almond flour

¼ cup (23 g) coconut flour

½ cup (120 ml) your favorite homemade marinara sauce, reserve 2 tbsp (30 ml) for topping

½ tsp sea salt

½ tsp black pepper

1 tbsp (15 ml) Worcestershire sauce

1 tsp Italian seasoning

½ tsp dried tarragon

½ cup (30 g) fresh flat leaf parsley, reserve 1 tbsp (4 g) for garnish

1 cup (240 ml) water

In a large mixing bowl, combine all of the ingredients except the water and mix well.

Transfer the mixture to a loaf pan big enough to fit into the inner pot of the Instant Pot. Cover the top of the meatloaf mixture with 2 tablespoons (30 ml) of marinara sauce. Loosely cover the pan with aluminum foil. Put the water in the inner pot and place the trivet inside. Place the pan containing the meatloaf mixture on top of the trivet.

Close the lid tightly and move the steam release handle to "Sealing."

Press the "Pressure Cooker/Manual" button and set the timer for 30 minutes on HIGH pressure. When the timer ends, you will hear a beeping sound. Allow the Instant Pot to cool down naturally until the float valve drops down. Press "Cancel" and open the lid. Carefully take out the trivet with the pan on top and let the meatloaf rest for 5 minutes. Serve immediately with Nourishing Cauli Mash (page 164) and garnish with the remaining fresh parsley.

*Nutrition:* Per Serving: 260 calories; 17g fat; 20g protein; 7g total carbohydrate; 3g dietary fiber

# Texas-Style BBQ Baby Back Ribs

One of my friends used to make baby back ribs every summer and his secret was to bake the ribs in a covered roasting pan on low heat for half the day. Then, he'd grill them on high heat, smothered in store-bought BBQ sauce before serving. Well, I can clearly beat him in his game by using the Instant Pot to make even better baby back ribs that fall off the bones in under an hour. And these are even more flavorful than any of the ribs you get with other conventional methods. Brown the ribs under the broiler or on the outdoor BBQ grill and smother it with your own sugar-free BBQ sauce before serving these finger-licking ribs!

*Cook Time: 25 minutes // Servings: 6*

### DRY RUB

2 tbsp (14 g) chili powder

½ cup (120 g) dry sweetener of your choice (I use Swerve)

¼ cup (122 g) sea salt

1 tbsp (7 g) black pepper

2 tbsp (14 g) dry mustard

2 tbsp (14 g) cumin

1 tbsp (7 g) garlic powder

1 tbsp (7 g) onion powder

1 tbsp (7 g) paprika

1 tsp cayenne pepper

1 tsp dried oregano

1 tsp celery seeds

2 tsp (5 g) turmeric

### RIBS

2 full racks of baby back ribs (~5 lbs [2.27 kg])

1 cup (240 ml) water

½ cup (120 ml) apple cider vinegar (ACV)

2 thumb-length ginger roots (~2 oz [57 g]), sliced in half, vertically

### BBQ SAUCE

¼ cup (60 ml) tomato sauce

2 tbsp (32 g) tomato paste

¼ cup (60 ml) apple cider vinegar (ACV)

2 tbsp (30 ml) liquid smoke

1 tbsp (15 ml) Worcestershire sauce

1 tbsp (15 g) sweetener of your choice

1 tbsp (15 g) dry rub (see left)

1 tbsp (8 g) tapioca flour (optional)

(continued)

Make the dry rub by mixing the spices and herbs in a small mixing bowl and set aside.

Put the ribs on a cutting board and using a paper towel, take the membrane off from the bony side of the ribs. This will allow more flavor to be infused into the meat. Repeat with the second rack. Cut the racks in half so they can fit in the inner pot. Sprinkle the dry rub all over the ribs and put them in zip-top bags to marinate overnight in the refrigerator. Reserve at least 1 tablespoon (15 g) of the dry rub to be used in the BBQ sauce later.

When it's time to cook the next day, take the ribs out of the refrigerator and let them rest at room temperature while you prepare the Instant Pot. Put the water, ACV and ginger in the inner pot. Stand the 4 half racks of ribs on their bony ends in the inner pot. You should be able to fit all the ribs in the pot in this fashion.

Press the "Pressure Cooker/Manual" button and set the timer for 16 minutes (a bit chewy) or 25 minutes (fall-off-the-bone). Close the lid tightly and move the steam release handle to "Sealing."

Meanwhile, make the BBQ sauce by combining the BBQ sauce ingredients in a small saucepan. Bring to boil and simmer for 5 minutes and set aside.

When the timer goes off in the Instant Pot, the setting will switch to "Warm." Wait until the time on the panel goes up to 5 minutes, and carefully turn the steam release handle to the "Venting" position for the steam to escape and the float valve to drop down. Press "Cancel."

Meanwhile, turn the oven to broil. Open the lid on the Instant Pot and take the ribs out and brush with the BBQ sauce on both sides. Place the ribs on a roasting pan and broil each side for 4 to 5 minutes or until browned. You can also brown them on the outdoor grill instead. Brush with more sauce if needed before serving.

---

*Nutrition:* Per Serving: 690 calories; 56g fat; 39g protein; 7g total carbohydrate; 1g dietary fiber

---

**Note:** If you want a thick BBQ sauce on the ribs while eating, you can add 1 tablespoon (8 g) of tapioca flour to the sauce and stir for 2 minutes to thicken it. But if you want to brush it on before putting them under the broiler, then you can skip the tapioca flour. It will reduce the carb content without it.

# Low-Carb Swedish Meatballs

Who else loves Swedish meatballs at the popular Swedish home mega-store, but hates to go there? Don't worry. You don't have to make a special trip to the store to have this quintessential Swedish dish. In fact, you could make dozens of these delicious meatballs in less time than it takes you to get on the turnpike! But if you need help getting that bookcase assembled, you won't find any help here. Sorry.

*Cooking Time: 23 minutes // Servings: 4*

1 lb (450 g) ground beef

1 cup (154 g) yellow onion, diced, reserve ½ cup (77 g) for sauce

¼ cup (15 g) fresh flat leaf parsley, chopped, reserve 2 tbsp (8 g) for garnish

1 large egg, beaten

2 tbsp (19 g) garlic, finely minced

1 tsp sea salt

1 tsp black pepper

½ tsp ground nutmeg, divided

¼ tsp ground allspice

2 tbsp (16 g) tapioca flour, divided

2 tbsp (30 g) butter

1 cup (240 ml) beef stock

½ cup (120 ml) full-fat heavy cream

¼ tsp sea salt

¼ tsp white pepper

½ cup (60 g) full-fat sour cream

In a medium-sized mixing bowl, combine the ground beef, ½ cup (77 g) of the diced onion, ¼ cup (15 g) of parsley, the beaten egg, garlic, sea salt, black pepper, half of the nutmeg, allspice and 1 tablespoon (8 g) of tapioca flour, and mix well. Form 1- to 1½-inch (2.5- to 3.75-cm) balls and set aside.

Turn on the Instant Pot by pressing "Sauté" and set to "More." Insert the inner pot and wait until the panel says "Hot." Melt the butter in the inner pot and sauté the remaining onion for 2 minutes. Add half of the meatballs and brown for 2 minutes. Take out the first batch and brown the second for 2 minutes. When all the meatballs are browned, add the first batch back to the inner pot and add the beef stock.

Close the lid tightly and move the steam release handle to "Sealing." Press "Cancel," then press the "Pressure Cooker/Manual" button and set the timer for 15 minutes on HIGH pressure. When the timer ends, you will hear a beeping sound. Allow the Instant Pot to cool down naturally until the float valve drops down. Press "Cancel," then "Sauté" and open the lid. Add the remaining tapioca flour, heavy cream, sea salt, white pepper, sour cream and the remaining ground nutmeg to the pot and stir for 2 minutes or until the sauce bubbles and thickens. If you like a thicker sauce, add more tapioca flour and stir. Press "Cancel." Serve immediately with the remaining chopped parsley. You can serve with Nourishing Cauli Mash (page 164) or zoodles.

---

*Nutrition:* Per Serving: 157 calories; 14g fat; 6g protein; 3g total carbohydrate; trace dietary fiber

# Roasted Brussels Sprouts with Bacon and Almonds

Brussels sprouts get a bad rep. But add bacon and, suddenly, they are popular. And what's even better? Cooking them in the Instant Pot! They come nicely browned on the outside, soft on the inside. You won't even know or care that they're low carb!

*Cook Time: 15 minutes // Servings: 4*

1 lb (450 kg) fresh Brussels sprouts (1–1 ½ inch [2.5–3.75 cm] in size)

1 tsp sea salt

1 tsp garlic powder

1 tbsp (15 g) butter

1 small onion, diced

2 cloves garlic, crushed

3 strips uncured bacon, cut into ½-inch (12-mm) pieces

1 tbsp (7 g) extra fine blanched almond slivers

½ cup (120 ml) chicken broth

2 tbsp (6 g) scallions, chopped, for garnish

**Note:** If you don't want to take the time to brown the Brussels sprouts, cook them in the Instant Pot for 10 minutes under high pressure first and then, roast under the broiler.

If the Brussels sprouts are smaller than 1 inch (2.5 cm) in diameter, reduce the cooking time to 5 minutes under HIGH pressure to prevent overcooking them.

Wash the Brussels sprouts well and discard any old and rotten leaves. Trim the ends off and cut the Brussels sprouts in half vertically. Put any loose leaves with the rest of the Brussels sprouts, sea salt and garlic powder in a large mixing bowl and mix.

Turn on the Instant Pot by pressing "Sauté" and set to "More." Insert the inner pot and wait until the panel says "Hot."

Add the butter, onion and garlic and sauté for 2 minutes or until the onion is soft. Add the bacon and sauté for 3 minutes or until the bacon starts to shrivel. If there's too much bacon grease, you can spoon out some of it now. You want some bacon grease, but not so much that the Brussels sprouts won't brown.

Push the bacon to the side and add half of the Brussels sprouts to brown. Place the Brussels sprouts with their flat sides down on the inner pot. Do not to crowd them and don't mix until the sides turn brown.

When most of the sides are browned, take them out, place them in a bowl and set aside. Add the remaining Brussels sprouts to the inner pot to brown the sides. If needed, add more bacon grease back so as not to burn the Brussels sprouts. When they are browned, add the first batch of the browned Brussels sprouts back to the inner pot and add the almonds and the chicken broth and mix while scraping the bottom of the inner pot to loosen up all the bits and pieces.

Hit "Cancel," then press the "Pressure Cooker/Manual" button and set the timer for 8 minutes on HIGH pressure.

Close the lid tightly and move the steam release handle to "Sealing." When the timer goes off, turn the steam release handle to the "Venting" position carefully for the steam to escape and the float valve to drop down. Press "Cancel." Open the lid.

Garnish with the chopped scallions and serve immediately with Texas-Style BBQ Baby Back Ribs (page 97).

*Nutrition:* Per Serving: 128 calories; 6g fat; 7g protein; 14g total carbohydrate; 5g dietary fiber

# Braised Collard Greens with Ham Hocks

"Collards," or "greens" as they say in the South, are a classic vegetable side dish to serve with BBQ meats. Braised with ham hocks, they usually take half a day to make. But not in the Instant Pot. Make these and serve them with Texas-Style BBQ Baby Back Ribs (page 97). I guarantee that they will go as fast as the ribs.

*Cooking Time: 20 minutes // Servings: 4*

**3 strips uncured bacon, chopped into 1-inch (2.5-cm) pieces**

**1 medium onion, diced**

**5 cloves garlic, crushed**

**2 lbs (900 g) collard greens, stems removed**

**2 lbs (900 g) smoked ham hock**

**1 tsp liquid smoke**

**1 tbsp (15 ml) apple cider vinegar (ACV)**

**2 dried whole bay leaves**

**Juice from 1 lemon and its zest**

**½ cup (30 g) chopped fresh flat leaf parsley, reserve 1 tbsp (4 g) for garnish**

Turn on the Instant Pot by pressing "Sauté" and set to "More." Insert the inner pot and wait until the panel says "Hot." Add the bacon to the inner pot of the Instant Pot. Sauté for 5 minutes or until the bacon browns around the edges. Add the onion and garlic and sauté for 2 minutes until the onion is soft. Add the remaining ingredients except for the 1 tablespoon (4 g) of parsley.

Close the lid tightly and move the steam release handle to "Sealing."

Press "Cancel," then the "Pressure Cooker/Manual" button and set the timer for 20 minutes on HIGH pressure. When the timer ends, you will hear a beeping sound. Allow the Instant Pot to cool down naturally until the float valve drops down. Press "Cancel" and open the lid. Serve immediately with the remaining parsley as a garnish.

*Nutrition:* Per Serving: 511 calories; 26g fat; 51g protein; 12g total carbohydrate; 6g dietary fiber

# Mongolian Beef

I really don't know if this recipe really is from Mongolia, but regardless of where it originated, this delicious and sultry meat dish is one of my favorites. It pairs well with any steamed vegetables and over Cauli Couscous (page 152), too!

*Cooking Time: 18 minutes // Servings: 6*

2 lbs (900 kg) flank steak or brisket, sliced ½-inch (13-mm) thick, 2 x 1-inch (5 x 2.5-cm) strips

½ tsp sea salt

½ tsp black pepper

6 cloves garlic, minced, divided

1 tbsp (15 ml) avocado oil

¼ cup (60 ml) tamari or coconut aminos

1 tsp minced fresh ginger

1 tbsp (15 g) dry sweetener (I use Swerve)

½ cup (120 ml) water, divided

2 tbsp (16 g) tapioca flour

½ cup (25 g) scallions, chopped into 1-inch (2.5-cm) pieces

In a small bowl, combine the beef, sea salt, black pepper and 1 teaspoon of minced garlic. Set aside. Turn on the Instant Pot by pressing "Sauté" and set to "More." Insert the inner pot and wait until the panel says "Hot." Add the avocado oil into the pot and heat until hot. Add half of the beef and sauté for 3 minutes or until the meat is no longer pink. Take out the browned beef and add the other batch of beef to brown. When all of the beef is browned, add the first batch back to the pot with its juices and the rest of the ingredients, except ¼ cup (60 ml) of water, the tapioca flour and the scallions.

Close the lid tightly and move the steam release handle to "Sealing." Press "Cancel," then the "Pressure Cooker/Manual" button and set the timer for 10 minutes on HIGH pressure. Mix the remaining water and the tapioca in a small bowl to make a slurry.

When the timer ends, you will hear a beeping sound. Allow the Instant Pot to cool down naturally until the float valve drops down. Press "Cancel," then "Sauté," and open the lid. Add the slurry and stir to thicken and simmer for 2 minutes. Press "Cancel." Serve immediately over Cauli Couscous (page 152) with the chopped scallions as garnish.

---

*Nutrition:* Per Serving: 310 calories; 18g fat; 31g protein; 4g total carbohydrate; trace dietary fiber

---

# Chorizo-Stuffed Artichokes

The first time I had stuffed artichokes was in college when my Italian roommate brought them from home. Before then, I never had artichokes, let alone artichokes stuffed with perfectly-seasoned Italian sausage and breadcrumbs. She showed me how to scrape the ends of the leaves and then, how to finally get to the soft heart. I admit, it was fun and messy to eat through the layers and oh-so-memorable. So of course, I had to modify the recipe to be Keto-friendly without grains and sugar. Serve them as appetizers or as a light lunch!

*Cooking Time: 30 minutes // Servings: 8*

4 artichokes, 2–3-inches (5–7.5 cm) in diameter

1 small onion, quartered

1 small carrot, quartered

2 large eggs

1 cup (182 g) grated Parmesan cheese, reserve 1 tbsp (11 g) for garnish

½ cup (49 g) extra fine blanched almond flour

½ lb (227 g) ground chorizo sausage

½ cup (120 ml) water

½ cup (120 ml) extra-virgin olive oil (EVOO)

1 tbsp (4 g) chopped flat leaf parsley, for garnish

Wash each artichoke in water and discard any old or browned leaves. Cut the stem as close to the flower straight across and make sure it can sit on a flat surface. With kitchen scissors, cut the pointy ends of the leaves, leaving enough of the leaves to hold the filling. Using a sharp kitchen knife, cut the top ends flat across. When all four artichokes are prepped, set them aside and cover with a wet paper towel until ready to be stuffed.

In a food processor, add the onion, carrot and eggs, and blend. Add the cheese and flour and process until they are mixed well. Add the chorizo and blend but do not overblend.

Separate each leaf of the artichoke and, with a small spoon, stuff with the sausage filling. When all of them are stuffed, pour the water and EVOO into the inner pot of the Instant Pot. Place the artichokes on the bottom of the inner pot. You should be able to put two on the bottom and the other two on top, scattered. Place the inner pot in the Instant Pot and close the lid tightly and move the steam release handle to "Sealing." Press the "Pressure Cooker/Manual" button and set the timer for 30 minutes on HIGH pressure.

When you hear the beeping sound indicating that the time ended, carefully turn the steam release handle to the "Venting" position for the steam to escape and the float valve to drop down. Press "Cancel," and open the lid carefully. Remove the artichokes to a plate, sprinkle the remaining Parmesan cheese on top, garnish with the parsley and serve immediately.

*Nutrition:* Per Serving: 252 calories; 18g fat; 14g protein; 8g total carbohydrate; 2g dietary fiber

# Carnitas for Every Day

Carnitas is a popular dish for many reasons but using it in lettuce wraps and over Lime Cilantro Cauli Couscous (page 152) is my favorite way to eat it. If you want to make a drier version, put it under the broiler for a couple of minutes and squeeze lime juice over the top. It's great on salads too!

*Cooking Time: 30 minutes // Servings: 8*

1 (3-lb [1.4-kg]) skinless picnic shoulder pork, cut to fit the pot

1 tsp black pepper

1½ tsp (8 g) dry adobo seasoning

½ tsp garlic powder

1 tbsp (7 g) cumin, divided

6 cloves garlic, crushed

½ cup (120 ml) bone broth

½ cup (120 ml) tomato sauce

1 small onion, chopped

2 jalapeños, sliced

½ tbsp (1 g) dried oregano

2 dried whole bay leaves

3 limes, 2 juiced and 1 cut into 8 wedges, for garnish

¼ cup (4 g) chopped fresh cilantro, reserve 2 tbsp (2 g) for garnish

Pat the pork dry and rub the sides with the black pepper, adobo seasoning, garlic powder and 2 teaspoons (5 g) of cumin. Set aside.

Turn on the Instant Pot by pressing the "Pressure Cooker/Manual" button and set the timer for 30 minutes on HIGH pressure.

Add the pork shoulder and the remaining ingredients, except for the lime wedges and 2 tablespoons (2 g) of cilantro into the inner pot. Close the lid tightly and move the steam release handle to "Sealing." When the timer ends, you will hear a beeping sound. Allow the Instant Pot to cool down naturally until the float valve drops down. Press "Cancel" and open the lid.

Remove the pork and pull the meat apart with a fork. Serve immediately with lime wedges and the remaining cilantro over Lime Cilantro Cauli Couscous (page 152).

---

*Nutrition:* Per Serving: 337 calories; 24g fat; 24g protein; 7g total carbohydrate; 1g dietary fiber

---

Note: If you prefer drier and crispier carnitas, pull the meat apart a little and place it under the broiler for a few minutes until the liquid dries. Squeeze lime juice on top and serve immediately.

# Barbacoa for the Crowd

Who doesn't love rich-flavored beef that you can eat with just about anything? That's how this recipe is. You can make this large batch of barbacoa and use it for many different recipes. Serve with Lime Cilantro Cauli Couscous (page 152) or in a taco or burrito bowl. The possibilities are endless!

*Cooking Time: 40 minutes // Servings: 12*

1 (4-lb [1.8-kg]) eye round roast or chuck roast

1 lb (450 g) oxtail bones

1 tsp sea salt

1 tsp black pepper

2 tbsp (30 ml) extra virgin olive oil (EVOO)

1 small onion, chopped

6 medium cloves garlic, crushed

2 cups (480 ml) beef stock or broth

2 tsp (4 g) ground cumin

½ tsp ground coriander

2 tsp (4 g) dried oregano

½ tsp cinnamon

1 tsp whole cloves

1 (7-oz [198-g]) can of chipotle chili peppers in adobo sauce

1 tbsp (15 ml) apple cider vinegar (ACV)

1 bell pepper, chopped

2 dried whole bay leaves

1 bunch of chopped fresh cilantro, reserve 2 tbsp (2 g) for garnish

Pat the meat and oxtail bones dry and season them with the sea salt and black pepper. Turn on the Instant Pot by pressing "Sauté" and set to "More." Insert the inner pot and wait until the panel says "Hot." Add the EVOO and, when it gets hot, add the meat in batches and brown the surfaces for 3 minutes on each side. Remove the browned meat and set aside. Sauté the onion and garlic for 2 minutes or until the onion is soft. Add the meat and the remaining ingredients, except for 2 tablespoons (2 g) of cilantro, to the inner pot. Close the lid tightly and move the steam release handle to "Sealing."

Press "Cancel," then the "Pressure Cooker/Manual" button and set the timer for 40 minutes on HIGH pressure. When the timer ends, you will hear a beeping sound. Allow the Instant Pot to cool down naturally until the float valve drops down. Press "Cancel" and open the lid. Debone the oxtail bones and put the meat back in the pot. You can serve immediately with the remaining cilantro as a garnish or marinate the meat in the sauce overnight and serve a day later for more flavor. Serve over Cilantro Cauli Couscous (page 152) or as a burrito bowl with all of the toppings.

---

*Nutrition:* Per Serving: 584 calories; 48g fat; 33g protein; 3g total carbohydrate; 1g dietary fiber

Note: This recipe freezes well too, so make a large batch and freeze half for later.

# Mexican Stuffed Peppers

My family normally doesn't like stuffed peppers, but they devour this Mexican-flavored version. These are quick to make, especially if you prepare the filling in advance. The only problem is that I need to make two batches since they love them so much. It could be worse, right?

*Cooking Time: 10 minutes // Servings: 4*

2 tbsp (30 ml) extra-virgin olive oil (EVOO)

1 small onion, diced

3 cloves garlic, pressed or minced

½ lb (227 g) ground chorizo sausage

1 cup (100 g) cooked Cauli Couscous (page 152)

3 small tomatoes, diced

½ tsp cumin

½ tsp garlic powder

½ tsp sea salt

1 tbsp (16 g) tomato paste

1 tsp chili powder

¼ cup (4 g) chopped fresh cilantro, reserve 1 tbsp (1 g) for garnish

4 bell peppers, any color

1 cup (240 ml) water

¼ cup (30 g) grated cheddar cheese, for garnish

Turn on the Instant Pot by pressing "Sauté" and set to "More." Insert the inner pot and wait until the panel says "Hot." Add the EVOO and heat until it's hot. Add the onion and garlic and sauté until the onion is soft. Add the sausage and sauté for 5 minutes or until the meat is separated. Add the rest of the ingredients except for the bell peppers, water and cheese, and stir. Remove the sausage mixture into a large mixing bowl and set aside. Wash the bell peppers, cut the tops and remove the stem and seeds. Fill each pepper with the sausage mixture, without overfilling to above the top of the peppers. Put the water in the inner pot, place the trivet inside and carefully place the filled peppers on the trivet.

Close the lid tightly and move the steam release handle to "Sealing." Press the "Pressure Cooker/Manual" button and set the timer for 10 minutes on HIGH pressure.

When you hear the beeping sound indicating that the time has ended, carefully turn the steam release handle to the "Venting" position for the steam to escape and the float valve to drop down. Press "Cancel," and open the lid carefully. Sprinkle grated cheddar cheese on top of each pepper and close the lid. Let the cheese melt for 3 to 5 minutes. Garnish with the remaining cilantro and serve immediately.

---

*Nutrition:* Per Serving: 338 calories; 22g fat; 17g protein; 19g total carbohydrate; 4g dietary fiber

---

# Fat-Packed Feathers

Occasionally, I crave chicken, especially after having red meat three days in a row. But my favorite part is still the fattier dark meat, hands down. Chicken breast meat has its purpose, like in the Asian Chicken Salad with Miso Dressing (page 133) or for Chicken Roulade with Creamy Artichoke Hearts (page 125) but for the most part, I love cooking with dark meat for its flavor and tenderness. But if you love white meat, by all means, you can make any of these recipes with lighter meat. No discrimination there, even if I state "chicken thighs" in the recipe. The advantage of cooking chicken in the Instant Pot is that it never comes out dry if you follow the instructions.

So, do you prefer white or dark meat? Regardless, you will love these protein-packed recipes with rich flavors!

# Everyday Chicken with Gravy

A whole roasted chicken is very versatile, and I like to make one weekly. However, it takes over an hour in the oven and it's not fail-proof. But not in the Instant Pot! It's easy and the chicken always comes out perfect. Make this regularly in the Instant Pot and use it in a variety of dishes throughout the week! Or serve it with low-carb gravy!

*Cooking Time: 40 minutes // Servings: 4*

1 tbsp (15 g) sea salt

1 tsp black pepper

1 tsp paprika

4 lbs (1.8 kg) whole chicken

4 tbsp (60 ml) lemon juice

2 tbsp (30 ml) melted butter

1 medium onion, sliced ½-inch (1.3-cm) thick

2 small celery stalks, cut into 1-inch (2.5-cm) pieces

1 small carrot, cut into 1-inch (2.5-cm) pieces

1 cup (240 ml) water

3 cloves garlic, crushed

1 (1-inch [2.5-cm]) piece fresh ginger, sliced

1 tbsp (7 g) dried oregano

1 tbsp (7 g) dried thyme

1 tbsp (7 g) dried rosemary

2 dried whole bay leaves

Giblets and chicken feet (optional)

1 bunch fresh flat leaf parsley, roughly chopped, reserve 1 tbsp (4 g) for garnish

1 tbsp (8 g) tapioca flour

Turn on the Instant Pot by pressing "Sauté" and set to "More." Insert the inner pot. Meanwhile, in a small bowl, combine the sea salt, black pepper and paprika, and divide the mixture in half. Lightly rub the chicken inside and out with the lemon juice and half of the sea salt and pepper mixture. Brush the chicken with the melted butter. When the panel says "Hot," put the chicken in the inner pot, breast side down. Sear the skin until it turns brown. It should take about 5 minutes. Remove the chicken to a platter. Add the vegetables, water, herbs and remaining salt mixture, except for 1 tablespoon (4 g) of parsley. If giblets and other chicken parts came with the chicken, put them with the vegetables in the pot. Place the chicken on top of the vegetables in the bottom of the pot, breast side up. If you have a trivet, you can place the trivet in the pot and place the chicken on top of the trivet for an easier time removing the chicken after it's cooked.

Close the lid tightly and move the steam release handle to "Sealing." Press "Cancel," then press the "Pressure Cooker/Manual" button and set the timer for 35 minutes on HIGH pressure. When the timer ends, you will hear a beeping sound. Allow the Instant Pot to cool down naturally until the float valve drops down. Press "Cancel" and open the lid.

Remove the chicken and serve it as is, or debone the chicken to be used in other dishes. For crispy skin, cook the chicken in the Instant Pot first, then place the chicken under the broiler for a few minutes.

Add the tapioca flour to the cooking liquid and whisk to thicken to make gravy to serve over the chicken.

After cooking, save the chicken carcass, vegetables and the cooking liquid in the pot to make broth or stock.

*Nutrition:* Per Serving: 1166 calories; 68g fat; 125g protein; 8g total carbohydrate; 1g dietary fiber

Note: In general, a whole chicken is cooked at 8 minutes per pound (450 g). For frozen chickens, the cooking time is 13 minutes per pound (450 g). Make sure there are no plastic bags of gizzards or parts inside the cavity before putting it in the Instant Pot.

# Spicy Mediterranean Chicken

The briny olives make this chicken very flavorful, but the heat from the cherry peppers makes this dish one of our favorites. If you don't like the "heat," you can leave out the cherry peppers, but I think it changes the flavor if you do. Take a chance. Try this delicious chicken with a little heat.

*Cooking Time: 15 minutes // Servings: 5*

1 small onion, chopped

2 cloves garlic, crushed

1 bell pepper, seeded and chopped

1 cup (180 g) diced tomatoes

3 lbs (1.4 kg) boneless chicken breasts and thighs

1 tsp smoked paprika

2 tbsp (8 g) chopped fresh flat leaf parsley, reserve 1 tbsp (4 g) for garnish

1 cup (182 g) green olives, pitted and sliced

½ cup (70 g) hot cherry pepper slices (in water)

¼ cup (60 ml) chicken broth or bone broth

¼ cup (60 ml) white wine

½ tsp sea salt or to taste

½ tsp black pepper

Place the onion, garlic, pepper and tomatoes into the Instant Pot and add the chicken on top. Add the herbs and spices on top, except for 1 tablespoon (4 g) of parsley. Then add the olives, hot cherry pepper slices, chicken broth and white wine.

Close the lid tightly and move the steam release handle to "Sealing."

Press "Cancel," then the "Pressure Cooker/Manual" button and set the timer for 15 minutes on HIGH pressure. When the timer ends, you will hear a beeping sound. Allow the Instant Pot to cool down naturally until the float valve drops down. Press "Cancel" and open the lid. Remove the chicken and vegetables to serving plates. Add sea salt and pepper to taste, garnish with parsley and serve immediately.

*Nutrition:* Per Serving: 444 calories; 23g fat; 47g protein; 8g total carbohydrate; 2g dietary fiber

# Buffalo-Style Chicken Wings

I went to college in upstate New York, where Buffalo chicken wings were like candy to the locals. There wasn't one person who didn't make or eat these spicy chicken wings. It took me a few years to eat them again, as I got so tired of them. But now, my family's favorite pastime is eating these wings while watching movies. And what's better than a healthy homemade version made in the Instant Pot without deep frying?

*Cooking Time: 15 minutes // Servings: 12*

2 cups (480 ml) hot sauce

¼ cup (60 ml) apple cider vinegar (ACV)

1 tbsp (7 g) cayenne pepper

½ cup (116 g) butter, melted

1 tsp sea salt

1 tsp black pepper

5 lbs (2.3 kg) chicken wings

In a medium-sized mixing bowl, combine the hot sauce, vinegar, cayenne pepper, butter, sea salt and black pepper, and whisk together. Reserve about ½ cup (120 ml) of the sauce for basting later. Remove the wing tips from the main wingettes and separate the drummettes. In the inner pot of the Instant Pot, combine the chicken wings and sauce and mix well. You can make the recipe up to this point and marinate overnight.

When ready to cook, turn on the Instant Pot by pressing the "Pressure Cooker/ Manual" button and set the timer for 10 minutes on HIGH pressure. Close the lid tightly and move the steam release handle to "Sealing."

When the timer ends, you will hear a beeping sound. Allow the Instant Pot to cool down naturally until the float valve drops down. Meanwhile, turn on the oven to broil.

Press "Cancel" on the Instant Pot and open the lid. Take out the chicken wings and place them in a single layer on a roasting pan. Baste the chicken wings with the reserved hot sauce. Broil for about 1 minute or until browned, without burning them. Mix the wings with more hot sauce and serve immediately.

*Nutrition:* Per Serving: 301 calories; 24g fat; 19g protein; 1g total carbohydrate; 1g dietary fiber

Note: If you need more sauce for basting, double the recipe and baste liberally when putting them under the broiler. Add more hot sauce if you want spicier wings. Serve with carrots and celery sticks and blue cheese dressing on the side.

# Chicken Roulade with Creamy Artichoke Hearts

I love artichoke hearts and I try to cook with them as often as I can. Pairing them with chicken was an idea that came to me as I was making the Espresso Cheesecake (page 168) and trying to come up with ways to use up the leftover cream cheese. I find inspiration at the strangest times. Anyway, this recipe turned out so good that even my daughter, who's sensitive to dairy, loved it. And her skin stayed clean after devouring her serving! The Keto diet is doing amazing things for her health!

*Cooking Time: 20 minutes * Servings: 4*

4 (1-lb [450-g]) chicken breasts

2 tsp (10 g) sea salt

2 tsp (5 g) black pepper

½ cup (91 g) grated Parmesan cheese

½ cup (61 g) shredded mozzarella

1 cup (84 g) artichoke hearts, finely chopped

½ cup (60 g) full-fat sour cream

¼ cup (61 g) cream cheese

1 tsp garlic, minced

1 tsp finely diced onion

½ cup (86 g) finely diced hot cherry peppers

½ cup (30 g) fresh flat leaf parsley, reserve 2 tbsp (8 g) for garnish

1 cup (240 ml) water

Place the chicken breasts on a cutting board and cut across the middle of the breasts without cutting all the way through. Open up the piece like a butterfly and using a meat tenderizer, gently flatten out the meat. Repeat and flatten out all the breasts. Season the breasts with sea salt and pepper and set them aside.

In a medium-sized bowl, combine and mix the rest of the ingredients except for the 2 tablespoons (8 g) of parsley. Divide the mixture into four servings. Spread the mixture on a flattened chicken breast and roll it up, like a sushi roll. Repeat with the rest of the chicken breasts. Place the chicken breasts in a casserole dish, open side down. Cover with a lid or aluminum foil. Place the casserole dish on the trivet. Pour 1 cup (240 ml) of water in the pot and carefully lower the trivet inside.

Turn on the Instant Pot by pressing the "Pressure Cooker/Manual" button and set the timer for 20 minutes on HIGH pressure. Close the lid tightly and move the steam release handle to "Sealing."

When the timer ends, you will hear a beeping sound. Allow the Instant Pot to cool down naturally until the float valve drops down. Press "Cancel" and open the lid. Grab the handles of the trivet and take out the casserole dish. There will be condensation on top of the aluminum foil so be careful not to spill. Uncover and move the chicken breasts onto serving plates. Garnish with the reserved parsley and serve immediately.

*Nutrition:* Per Serving: 863 calories; 51g fat; 87g protein; 10g total carbohydrate; 3g dietary fiber

# Turkey Enchilada Casserole

When you have leftover turkey from the holidays, this is a great way to use it up. But this recipe is so good that you'll want to buy turkey breast just to make it. Promise.

*Cooking Time: 30 minutes // Servings: 4*

1 lb (450 g) turkey breast, cubed into 1-inch (2.5-cm) pieces

15 oz (430 g) enchilada sauce

½ cup (77 g) diced onion

1 tsp minced garlic

½ cup (91 g) black olives

½ cup (120 ml) full-fat heavy cream

½ cup (120 ml) chicken stock

2 jalapeño peppers, diced

1 tbsp (7 g) chili powder

3 cups (367 g) shredded cheddar cheese, divided

½ cup (8 g) chopped fresh cilantro, reserve 2 tbsp (2 g) for garnish

4 scallions, chopped, reserve half for garnish

1 tsp tapioca flour

1½ cups (360 ml) water, divided

In a large mixing bowl, combine all the ingredients except for 2 cups (240 g) of cheddar cheese, 2 tablespoons (2 g) of cilantro, half of the scallions, the tapioca flour and water. Stir and mix the filling. In a small bowl, mix the tapioca flour and ½ cup (120 ml) of water and stir into the filling mixture. In a casserole dish, pour half of the filling, then 1 cup (122 g) of cheddar cheese and the remaining filling. Cover with the lid, if available, or with aluminum foil. Place the dish on the trivet.

Turn on the Instant Pot by pressing the "Pressure Cooker/Manual" button and set the timer for 30 minutes on HIGH pressure. Pour 1 cup (240 ml) of water and carefully lower the trivet. Close the lid tightly and move the steam release handle to "Sealing." When the timer ends, you will hear a beeping sound. Allow the Instant Pot to cool down naturally until the float valve drops down. Meanwhile, turn the oven to broil. Press "Cancel" on the Instant Pot and open the lid. Carefully grab the handles and lift out the trivet. Uncover and sprinkle with the remaining cheddar cheese. Place the dish in the oven to broil for 2 minutes or until the cheese melts.

Serve immediately with the remaining scallions and cilantro as garnish.

---

*Nutrition:* Per Serving: 782 calories; 60g fat; 47g protein; 14g total carbohydrate; 3g dietary fiber

---

# Better Butter Chicken

I have to admit, it took me a few years before I started really enjoying Indian food. The Indian restaurants around me serve some of the most authentic dishes and it took a few tries to get to love them. But this dish was an exception. I immediately fell in love with butter chicken and haven't stopped making it. It's one of our favorite Indian dishes!

*Cooking Time: 20 minutes // Servings: 6*

1 tbsp (15 ml) avocado oil

1 cup (154 g) chopped onion

4 cloves garlic, mashed

2 tbsp (29 g) peeled grated fresh ginger

½ tsp turmeric

½ tsp cumin

½ tsp garam masala

1 tsp curry powder

1 (14-oz [400-g]) can diced tomatoes

1 tsp paprika

1 tsp cayenne pepper

1 cup (16 g) chopped fresh cilantro, reserve ¼ cup (4 g) for garnish

3 lbs (1.4 kg) of bone-in chicken thighs

½ cup (120 ml) chicken broth

½ cup (116 g) butter, cut in pieces

1 cup (240 ml) full-fat heavy cream

Sea salt, to taste

Turn on the Instant Pot by pressing "Sauté" and set to "More." Insert the inner pot and wait until the panel says "Hot." To the inner pot, add the avocado oil. Then, sauté the onion, garlic and ginger for 2 minutes or until the onion is soft. Add the turmeric, cumin, garam masala, curry powder, diced tomatoes, paprika, cayenne pepper and ¾ cup (12 g) of cilantro. Add the chicken thighs and the chicken broth and stir well. Make sure all the thighs are coated. Pat down the ingredients and close the lid tightly. Move the steam release handle to "Sealing."

Press "Cancel," then press the "Pressure Cooker/Manual" button and set the timer for 20 minutes on HIGH pressure.

When the timer ends, you will hear a beeping sound. Allow the Instant Pot to cool down naturally until the float valve drops down. Press "Cancel" and then "Sauté." Open the lid, add the butter pieces, heavy cream and sea salt to taste. Stir and simmer for 2 minutes. Press "Cancel." Serve immediately with the remaining cilantro as garnish.

---

*Nutrition:* Per Serving: 713 calories; 60g fat; 34g protein; 10g total carbohydrate; 2g dietary fiber

---

**Note:** You can substitute heavy cream with full-fat coconut cream and butter with ghee if you are avoiding dairy.

# BBQ Chicken Drumsticks

Who doesn't love drumsticks? My family fights over drumsticks when there are only two legs from one whole chicken. So I make these drumsticks whenever they want dark meat. We like spicy food, so this BBQ mix works for us, but you can adjust the heat level according to your taste. Make a batch of the dry rub in advance and store in an airtight container for a quick meal!

*Cooking Time: 20 minutes // Servings: 4*

**2 tbsp (14 g) paprika**

**1 tbsp (7 g) black pepper**

**1 tbsp (15 g) sea salt**

**1 tsp celery seeds**

**1 tsp cayenne pepper**

**1 tsp garlic powder**

**1 tsp dry mustard**

**1 tsp cumin**

**1 tsp dried oregano**

**1 tsp dried parsley**

**2 lbs (900 g) chicken drumsticks**

**1 cup (240 ml) water**

Combine all of the spices and herbs, mix and set aside. Sprinkle half of the rub on the drumsticks. Add 1 cup (240 ml) of water to the Instant Pot and place the trivet inside. Put the drumsticks on the trivet.

Turn on the Instant Pot by pressing the "Pressure Cooker/Manual" button and set the timer for 20 minutes on HIGH pressure. Close the lid tightly and move the steam release handle to "Sealing." Preheat the oven to broil.

When the timer ends, you will hear a beeping sound. Allow the Instant Pot to cool down naturally until the float valve drops down. Press "Cancel" and open the lid. Remove the drumsticks and coat them evenly with the rub.

Place the drumsticks on a roasting pan in a single layer. Broil the drumsticks for 2 minutes per side or until the skin is browned. Be careful not to burn them. Serve immediately.

*Nutrition:* Per Serving: 270 calories; 14g fat; 30g protein; 5g total carbohydrate; 2g dietary fiber

# Asian Chicken Salad with Miso Dressing

Salad is usually not that filling. Adding proteins like chicken is a great way to add more substance so you don't get hungry. This Asian Chicken Salad recipe is from a friend and I modified it to fit our eating style. Make a large batch of the chicken and add the lettuce later so it doesn't wilt.

*Cooking Time: 15 minutes / Servings: 6*

1 lb (450 g) chicken breasts

1 tsp sea salt

½ tsp black pepper

½ tsp garlic powder

¼ cup (60 ml) white wine

1 cup (240 ml) water

½ head iceberg lettuce, sliced ½-inch (13-mm) thick

1 carrot, julienned

1 small purple onion, diced

3 scallions, chopped, reserve 1 tbsp (6 g) for garnish

1 tbsp (8 g) grated fresh ginger

2 tbsp (30 ml) rice vinegar

2 tbsp (34 g) miso paste, light or dark

1 tbsp (15 ml) sesame oil

1½ tsp (8 ml) lime juice

¼ cup (28 g) blanched almond slivers, for garnish

1 tsp toasted sesame seeds, for garnish

Season the chicken breast with the sea salt, black pepper, garlic powder and white wine and set aside.

Turn on the Instant Pot by pressing the "Pressure Cooker/Manual" button and set the timer for 15 minutes on HIGH pressure. Put the water in the inner pot and place the trivet inside. Place the seasoned chicken breast in a shallow dish and place it on the trivet. Close the lid tightly and move the steam release handle to "Sealing."

Meanwhile, cut the vegetables and transfer them to a large salad bowl. In a small mixing bowl, combine and whisk the ginger, rice vinegar, miso, sesame oil and lime juice. When the timer of the Instant Pot ends, you will hear a beeping sound. Allow the Instant Pot to cool down naturally until the float valve drops down. Press "Cancel" and open the lid. Remove the dish and using a fork, shred the chicken. Let the chicken cool for 5 minutes and then add it to the salad bowl with the vegetables. Add the salad dressing and mix well. Serve with the almond slivers, sesame seeds and remaining scallions on top.

*Nutrition:* Per Serving: 207 calories; 12g fat; 16g protein; 9g total carbohydrate; 3g dietary fiber

# Salsa Verde Chicken

Green tomatillos, where have you been all my life? This recipe's heroic ingredient is the green tomato, which adds color and flavoring. Queso fresco adds another dimension to this Latin-inspired chicken dish, so make this tonight to impress your family or guests.

*Cooking Time: 17 minutes // Servings: 6*

5 small green tomatillos, halved

1 jalapeño, seeded and chopped, plus more if desired

1 tbsp (7 g) dried oregano

1 bunch fresh cilantro, chopped, reserve 2 tbsp (2 g) for garnish

5 cloves garlic, crushed

1 medium onion, chopped

½ cup (120 ml) chicken broth

2 lbs (900 g) chicken breasts (boneless and skinless) and bone-in chicken thighs

1 cup (129 g) queso fresco

½ cup (120 ml) full-fat heavy cream

In the inner pot of the Instant Pot, add the tomatillos, jalapeño, oregano, cilantro, garlic, onion and chicken broth, then nestle the chicken pieces in between.

Turn on the Instant Pot by pressing the "Pressure Cooker/Manual" button and set the timer for 15 minutes on HIGH pressure. Close the lid tightly and move the steam release handle to "Sealing."

When the timer ends, you will hear a beeping sound. Allow the Instant Pot to cool down naturally until the float valve drops down. Press "Cancel" and open the lid. Remove the chicken and shred it with a fork. Using an immersion blender or a standing blender, purée the sauce. Add the chicken and the sauce back to the inner pot. Press "Sauté" and add the queso fresco and heavy cream and stir. Simmer for 2 minutes or until the sauce bubbles. Press "Cancel." Serve immediately with the reserved cilantro as garnish.

*Nutrition:* Per Serving: 331 calories; 20g fat; 29g protein; 7g total carbohydrate; 1g dietary fiber

Note: If you know how to debone a chicken, you can use the breast and the chicken legs with thighs. Save the rest of the chicken for making chicken stock or broth.

# Creamy Chicken and Broccoli

Chicken and broccoli go so well together, don't they? Add a creamy sauce, and they melt in your mouth. I can't decide if I like the sauce or the chicken and broccoli more!

*Cooking Time: 15 minutes  Servings: 4*

6 slices uncured bacon, chopped

½ cup (120 ml) chicken broth

8 oz (227 g) full-fat cream cheese

½ cup (120 ml) full-fat buttermilk

2 lbs (900 g) boneless chicken breast, cut into 1-inch (2.5-cm) chunks

¼ cup (15 g) fresh flat leaf parsley, reserve 1 tbsp (4 g) for garnish

1 tsp dried tarragon

½ tsp dried dill weed

½ tsp dried basil

½ tsp Herbes de Provence

2 tsp (5 g) onion powder

1 tsp garlic powder

1 tsp sea salt

½ tsp black pepper

2 cups (181 g) broccoli florets

2 tbsp (18 g) blue cheese crumbles

Turn on the Instant Pot by pressing "Sauté" and set to "More." Insert the inner pot and wait until the panel says "Hot." Add the bacon pieces and sauté to brown, 3 minutes. Add the chicken broth and deglaze the bacon bits. Add the cream cheese and buttermilk, and stir. Add the chicken pieces and the rest of the ingredients except for the broccoli and 1 tablespoon (4 g) of parsley.

Close the lid tightly and move the steam release handle to "Sealing."

Press the "Pressure Cooker/Manual" button and set the timer for 15 minutes on HIGH pressure. When the timer goes off, allow the Instant Pot to cool down naturally until the float valve drops down and you can open the lid. After cooking is finished, press "Cancel." Add the broccoli and stir. Press "Pressure Cooker/Manual" and set the timer to "0" minutes.

When you hear the beeping sound indicating that the time has ended, carefully turn the steam release handle to the "Venting" position for the steam to escape and the float valve to drop down. Press "Cancel," and open the lid. Sprinkle blue cheese crumbles and garnish with remaining parsley before serving.

*Nutrition:* Per Serving: 545 calories; 28g fat; 64g protein; 7g total carbohydrate; 1g dietary fiber

# Satisfying Swimmers

Even though seafood is one of my favorites, I admit it is sometimes not as satiating since it's not as fatty as red meat. But with the addition of good healthy fats, seafood can be filling, just like any other type of meat. And with Ketogenic renditions of classic dishes like Grain-Free Lobster Mac and Cheese (page 140) and Easy-Peasy Seafood Paella (page 144), you will not miss all the carbs! In fact, these recipes may just become your family's favorites!

# Grain-Free Lobster Mac and Cheese

This Keto-fied version of mac and cheese is so good and so satisfying for anyone, Keto or not, you'll want to make huge batches of it. Make the lobster meat and the "cheese" ahead and assemble the rest of the ingredients for a quick meal that will become everyone's favorite!

*Cooking Time: 10 minutes // Servings: 4*

3 (1–1½ lb [450–680 g]) live lobsters (freeze two hours beforehand) OR 1½–2 lbs (680–900 g) cooked lobster tails

1 large cauliflower, cut into bite-size florets

6 oz (170 g) unsalted butter, divided

1 cup (240 ml) full-fat heavy whipping cream

2 cups (244 g) shredded medium sharp cheddar cheese, divided

2 cups (228 g) grated Gruyère cheese, divided

2 tsp (10 g) sea salt

1 tsp black pepper

¼ freshly ground nutmeg

1 tsp dry mustard powder

2 tbsp (16 g) tapioca flour

1 cup (240 ml) water

¼ cup (24 g) extra fine blanched almond flour, for topping

1 tbsp (4 g) fresh flat leaf parsley, chopped, for garnish

1 tsp paprika, for topping (optional)

*Nutrition:* Per Serving: 1258 calories; 103g fat; 68g protein; 16g total carbohydrate; 5g dietary fiber

Turn on the Instant Pot by pressing the "Pressure Cooker/Manual" button and set the timer for "0" minutes on HIGH pressure.

Cut and discard the outer leaves of the cauliflower and cut into florets. Put water in the inner pot and place the steamer basket inside. Put the florets in the steamer basket and close the lid tightly. Move the steam release handle to "Sealing." In a small mixing bowl, mix 4 ounces (114 g) of butter, the heavy whipping cream, half of the cheeses, sea salt, black pepper, nutmeg, mustard powder and tapioca flour, and set aside.

When you hear the beeping sound indicating that the time has ended, carefully turn the steam release handle to the "Venting" position for the steam to escape and the float valve to drop down. Open the lid carefully and remove the water and the steamer basket. Put the florets back in the inner pot. Add the cream and cheese mixture. If the sauce needs more thickening, add more tapioca and whisk together. Press "Cancel," and then "Sauté" to mix for 2 minutes or until the mixture bubbles.

Butter a deep casserole dish or a roasting pan with the remaining butter. Transfer the cauliflower mixture into the casserole dish or roasting pan, cover and set aside. Clean the inner pot and wipe the outside dry. Pour in 1 cup (240 ml) of water, place the trivet inside and place it in the Instant Pot. Press "Cancel."

Take out the lobsters from the freezer, clean the shells with a brush, and put them on a cutting board on their backs. With a sharp knife, pierce between the upper body and the lower body on top—where the head shell ends and the legs start—in one quick motion. This is the most humane way to kill the lobsters because they die instantly and the legs will go limp. Cut the lobster tails and set aside. Reserve the bodies for your other cooking needs.

Press the "Pressure Cooker/Manual" button on the Instant Pot and set the timer for 5 minutes on HIGH pressure. Place the lobster tails on the trivet and close the lid tightly and move the steam release handle to "Sealing." Preheat the oven to broil.

When the timer ends, you will hear a beeping sound. Allow the Instant Pot to cool down naturally until the float valve drops down. Press "Cancel" and open the lid. Take the lobster tails out to a cutting board. When they are cool enough to handle, using the end of a sharp knife, make a slit at the end of the lobster tail. Using your finger, push the meat out through the opposite end. Cut the lobster tail meat into bite-size chunks. Add them to the roasting pan with the cauliflower mixture and mix well. Sprinkle the remaining cheeses and almond flour on top. Place the pan under the broiler and brown for 1 to 2 minutes without burning the top. Sprinkle with the fresh parsley and paprika, if using, and serve immediately.

# Crab and Sundried Tomato Frittata

Crab frittata is really so easy to make that a child can cook it! Seriously. That's how simple it is. These are great to have for lunch, with a side of salad or even as breakfast! We love eating them at weekend brunches.

*Cooking Time: 10 minutes // Servings: 4*

2 lbs (900 g) lump crab meat

¼ cup (41 g) sun-dried tomatoes, chopped

¼ cup (15 g) chopped fresh flat leaf parsley, reserve 1 tsp for garnish

1 tbsp (7 g) dried tarragon

8 large eggs, beaten

1 cup (240 ml) almond milk, unsweetened

1 tsp sea salt

1 tsp black pepper

½ cup (61 g) shredded cheddar cheese, reserve 2 tbsp (15 g) for garnish

1 cup (240 g) water

In a medium-sized mixing bowl, combine all of the ingredients except for 1 teaspoon of parsley, 2 tablespoons (15 g) of cheddar cheese and the water. Transfer the mixture into 4 ramekins and cover with aluminum foil. Pour the water into the inner pot of the Instant Pot and place the trivet inside. Put the prepared ramekins on the trivet—2 on the bottom and 2 on the top, scattered.

Turn on the Instant Pot by pressing the "Pressure Cooker/Manual" button and set the timer for 10 minutes on HIGH pressure. Close the lid tightly and move the steam release handle to "Sealing."

When the timer ends, you will hear a beeping sound. Allow the Instant Pot to cool down naturally until the float valve drops down. Press "Cancel" and open the lid. Remove the ramekins, serve hot with the remaining shredded cheddar cheese and chopped parsley as a garnish.

*Nutrition:* Per Serving: 285 calories; 16g fat; 29g protein; 4g total carbohydrate; 1g dietary fiber

# Easy-Peasy Seafood Paella

Usually paella is made with rice, but when you make this Keto version, you won't even miss it. The rich seafood flavors are so delicious that you won't even think about other ingredients. And, it's quick to make in the Instant Pot so this may turn out to be your favorite seafood recipe.

*Cooking Times: 8 minutes // Servings: 6*

4 tbsp (60 ml) extra-virgin olive oil (EVOO)

1 medium onion, diced

1 red bell pepper, diced

1 green bell pepper, diced

1 lb (450 g) chorizo sausages, cut into 1-inch (2.5-cm) slices

1 cup (240 ml) fish stock or chicken broth

2 cups (250 g) cauliflower couscous

1 large pinch saffron threads

½ tsp ground turmeric

½ cup (30 g) chopped fresh flat leaf parsley, reserve 1 tbsp (4 g) for garnish

1 tsp black pepper

1 cup (112 g) seafood mix (squid, meaty white fish, scallops)

2 cups (320 g) mixed shellfish (clams, mussels, shrimp)

Turn on the Instant Pot by pressing "Sauté" and set to "More." Insert the inner pot and wait until the panel says "Hot." Heat the EVOO and sauté the onion and bell peppers for 3 minutes or until the vegetables are soft. Add the chorizo sausages and sauté for 3 minutes or until the surface is no longer pink. Add the fish stock or chicken broth, cauliflower couscous, saffron, turmeric, parsley and black pepper and mix. Add the seafood mixture, then place the shellfish on top. Do not mix.

Close the lid tightly and move the steam release handle to "Sealing." Press "Cancel," then the "Pressure Cooker/Manual" button and set the timer for 5 minutes on HIGH pressure.

When you hear the beeping sound indicating that the time has ended, carefully turn the steam release handle to the "Venting" position for the steam to escape and the float valve to drop down. Press "Cancel," and open the lid carefully. Serve immediately with the reserved parsley as garnish.

*Nutrition:* Per Serving: 473 calories; 39g fat; 20g protein; 9g total carbohydrate; 2g dietary fiber

# Salmon with Balsamic Glaze over Spinach

Salmon is one of the most nutritious fishes with omega-3 fatty acids, so I try to serve it as often as I can. And the Instant Pot helps me make this quick yet very tasty dish that even my children love.

*Cooking Time: 9 minutes // Servings: 4*

1–1½ lbs (450–680 g) wild-caught Pacific salmon

¼ cup (60 ml) balsamic vinegar, divided

1½ tsp (3 g) Herbes de Provence

1 tsp sea salt, divided

1 tsp black pepper, divided

1 cup (240 ml) water

2 tbsp (30 g) butter

2 cloves garlic, minced

2 lbs (900 g) baby spinach

2 tbsp (12 g) scallions, finely chopped, for garnish

Turn on the Instant Pot by pressing the "Pressure Cooker/Manual" button and set the timer for 5 minutes on HIGH pressure. Place the inner pot in the Instant Pot.

Cut the fish to fit inside the pot. Drizzle 1 tablespoon (15 ml) of the vinegar, Herbes de Provence, ½ teaspoon of sea salt and ½ teaspoon of black pepper on the flesh side of the fish. Put the water in the inner pot, place the trivet inside and place the fish on the trivet, flesh side up. Close the lid tightly and move the steam release handle to "Sealing." Meanwhile, turn the oven to broil and place a rack about 6 inches (15 cm) below the broiler.

When you hear the beeping sound from the Instant Pot, indicating that the time has ended, carefully turn the steam release handle to the "Venting" position for the steam to escape and the float valve to drop down. Press "Cancel," and open the lid carefully. Remove the salmon and the trivet. Place the salmon on a roasting pan and place it under the broiler in the oven and set the oven timer to 2 minutes.

Pour the liquid out of the inner pot and press "Sauté." Add the butter, ½ teaspoon of sea salt, ½ teaspoon of black pepper, the minced garlic and spinach. Sauté the spinach for 1 to 2 minutes or until just wilted. Remove the spinach and cooking liquid to a serving platter.

Add the remaining 3 tablespoons (45 ml) of balsamic vinegar to the inner pot and reduce until a thick glaze is formed, which should take less than 2 minutes. Press "Cancel" and leave the glaze inside until serving. Check on the salmon. If it's browned, take it out and place it on top of the spinach. If not, broil some more. Plate the browned salmon on top of the spinach, drizzle with balsamic glaze and garnish with the scallions before serving.

*Nutrition:* Per Serving: 239 calories; 10g fat; 29g protein; 10g total carbohydrate; 6g dietary fiber

**Note:** Browning the salmon in the oven is not required. If you want to skip it, you can just plate the salmon over the spinach and serve with the balsamic glaze.

# Coconut Curry Shrimp

My daughter is not a big fan of coconut-flavored foods. But she devoured this dish, as the creamy coconut milk and curry flavor made the shrimp so tasty that she didn't mind it at all. I call that a success!

*Cooking Time: 5 minutes // Servings: 4*

2 tbsp (30 g) butter

1 small onion, diced

1 tsp grated or finely minced ginger

1 clove garlic, minced or pressed

1 lb (450 g) shrimp with shells, deveined

1 tsp curry powder

½ cup (120 ml) water

¼ head cauliflower, florets and stems cut

½ cup (120 ml) full-fat coconut milk

½ tsp sea salt

1 tbsp (1 g) fresh cilantro, chopped, for garnish

1 tbsp (3 g) fresh scallions, chopped, for garnish

Turn on the Instant Pot by pressing "Sauté" and set to "More." Insert the inner pot and wait until the panel says "Hot." Add the butter to the inner pot and, when the butter melts, add the onion, ginger and garlic, and sauté for 2 minutes or until the onion is soft. Add the shrimp, curry powder and water. Close the lid tightly and move the steam release handle to "Sealing." Press the "Pressure Cooker/Manual" button and set the timer for 3 minutes on HIGH pressure.

When you hear the beeping sound indicating that the time has ended, carefully turn the steam release handle to the "Venting" position to let the steam escape until the float valve drops down. Press "Cancel," and open the lid carefully. Add the cauliflower, coconut milk and sea salt and close the lid tightly. Press the "Pressure Cooker/Manual" and set the timer for "0" minutes. When you hear the beeping sound indicating that time has ended, carefully turn the steam release handle to the "Venting" position and let the steam escape until the float valve drops down. Press "Cancel," and open the lid carefully. Garnish with the scallions and cilantro and serve immediately.

---

*Nutrition:* Per Serving: 265 calories; 15g fat; 25g protein; 8g total carbohydrate; 2g dietary fiber

---

# Green with Envy

As nourishing as meats are, we need greens in our diets, too. And they don't have to taste boring. What's great about Keto recipes is that greens can be rich and flavorful when you use the right ingredients. You can turn any vegetables into nutritious main dishes or sides.

Spaghetti Squash a la Vodka (page 155) can be served as a main meal or as a side dish, and Braised Collard Greens with Ham Hocks (page 105) make a great side to Texas-Style BBQ Baby Back Ribs (page 97). Plus, cooking vegetables in the Instant Pot takes little or no time at all, so you can focus on your main course!

# Cauli Couscous and Lime Cilantro Cauli Couscous

Cauliflower couscous, or cauli couscous, is a healthy substitute for any carb. It is easy to make and goes well with just about any meal. Add some cilantro and lime and you get a different side dish that complements certain dishes even better.

*Cooking Time: 0 minutes // Servings: 4*

**1 large head cauliflower**

**½ cup (120 ml) water**

Turn on the Instant Pot by pressing the "Pressure Cooker/Manual" button and set the timer for "0" minutes on HIGH pressure.

Cut the leaves and excess stem from the bottom of the cauliflower. Cut the florets and separate them from the stems. Wash the florets and drain the water.

Put the water in the inner pot and place the steamer basket inside. Put the cauliflower florets on the steamer basket. Close the lid tightly and move the steam release handle to "Sealing."

Meanwhile, fill a large mixing bowl with cold water. When you hear the beeping sound indicating that the time has ended, carefully turn the steam release handle to the "Venting" position for the steam to escape and the float valve to drop down. Press "Cancel," and open the lid. Remove the cauliflower and put it in the bowl with cold water to stop the cooking. The cauliflower should be thoroughly cooked but still crunchy enough to be used as a side dish. Put the florets in the food processor and pulse a few times. Don't overprocess.

*Nutrition:* Per Serving: 36 calories; trace fat; 3g protein; 7g total carbohydrate; 4g dietary fiber

**Note:** For Lime Cilantro Cauli Couscous, add ½ cup (8 g) of chopped cilantro and the juice from 1 lime to regular Cauli Couscous. Sprinkle with 1 teaspoon of sea salt and serve with a main course.

*Nutrition:* Per Serving: 28 calories; trace fat; 2g protein; 6g total carbohydrate; 2g dietary fiber

# Spaghetti Squash a la Vodka

Making spaghetti squash in the oven takes over an hour. But not in the Instant Pot! And what's even better is that you don't have to cut it to cook it! Try this method and serve the vodka sauce with it. You'll fall in love with spaghetti squash and the Instant Pot all over again.

*Cooking Time: 22 minutes / Servings: 4*

1 cup (240 ml) water

2 lbs (900 g) spaghetti squash

2 tbsp (30 ml) extra-virgin olive oil (EVOO)

1 small onion, finely chopped

6 cloves garlic, minced

1 cup (164 g) crushed tomatoes

2 tbsp (32 g) tomato paste

½ cup (120 ml) vodka

1 tsp sea salt

1 cup (240 ml) full-fat heavy whipped cream

½ cup (91 g) grated Parmesan cheese

¼ cup (30 g) chopped fresh flat leaf parsley, for garnish

Turn on the Instant Pot by pressing the "Pressure Cooker/Manual" button and set the timer for 15 minutes on HIGH pressure. Put the water in the inner pot and place the trivet inside. Poke a few holes in the spaghetti squash and place it on the trivet. Close the lid tightly and move the steam release handle to "Sealing."

When you hear the beeping sound indicating that the time has ended, carefully turn the steam release handle to the "Venting" position to let the steam escape until the float valve drops down. Press "Cancel," and open the lid carefully. Remove the trivet with the spaghetti squash and place it on a cutting board to cool.

Press "Sauté" on the Instant Pot and set to "Normal." Pour out the liquid from the inner pot and return it back to the Instant Pot. Add the EVOO and when the oil gets hot, add the onion and garlic and sauté for 2 minutes or until the onion is soft. Add the crushed tomatoes, tomato paste, vodka and salt. Simmer for 5 minutes.

Meanwhile, cut the spaghetti squash in half, crosswise. Using a fork, loosen up the inside into strands. Place them on a serving platter.

Press "Cancel" on the Instant Pot and open the lid. Add the heavy whipping cream and stir. Pour the vodka sauce over the spaghetti squash, sprinkle with the Parmesan cheese, garnish with chopped parsley and serve immediately.

*Nutrition:* Per Serving: 320 calories; 15g fat; 8g protein; 25g total carbohydrate; 5g dietary fiber

# Rich and Savory Cream of Kale

Kale is a great vegetable for a side; add some creamy sauce, and it's even better. This dish goes well with just about any meat dish, so try it with roasts and meatloaf. It'll temper spicy foods, too!

*Cooking Time: 5 minutes // Servings: 4*

2 tbsp (30 ml) extra-virgin olive oil (EVOO)

1 small onion, chopped

2 cloves garlic, crushed

12 oz (340 g) kale, finely chopped

1 tsp Herbes de Provence

½ cup (120 ml) chicken broth

4 oz (113 g) cream cheese

½ cup (120 ml) full-fat heavy cream

1 tsp dried tarragon

1 tsp tapioca flour

Turn on the Instant Pot by pressing "Sauté" and set to "More." Insert the inner pot and wait until the panel says "Hot." Add the EVOO to the inner pot. When the oil gets hot, add the onion and garlic and sauté for 2 minutes or until the onion is soft. Add the kale, Herbes de Provence and chicken broth, and stir.

Close the lid tightly and move the steam release handle to "Sealing." Press the "Pressure Cooker/Manual" button and set the timer for 3 minutes on HIGH pressure. Close the lid tightly and move the steam release handle to "Sealing."

When you hear the beeping sound indicating that the time has ended, carefully turn the steam release handle to the "Venting" position for the steam to escape and the float valve to drop down. Press "Cancel," and open the lid. Stir in the cream cheese, heavy cream, tarragon and tapioca flour. Stir well to thicken the sauce. Serve immediately.

*Nutrition:* Per Serving: 326 calories; 28g fat; 7g protein; 14g total carbohydrate; 2g dietary fiber

# Garlic-Roasted Buttery Whole Cauliflower

Roasted cauliflower is all the rage, but it takes almost an hour to roast in the oven. Luckily it takes practically no time to cook it in the Instant Pot first, then finish to a golden brown in the oven. The crispy roasted garlic adds deep flavor to the perfectly cooked cauliflower!

*Cooking Time: 8 minutes // Servings: 4*

**1 large cauliflower**

**1 cup (240 ml) water**

**4 tbsp (60 ml) melted butter**

**2 cloves of garlic, minced**

**Pinch of sea salt**

**Pinch of fresh ground black pepper**

**1 tbsp (4 g) chopped fresh flat leaf parsley, for garnish**

Turn on the Instant Pot by pressing the "Pressure Cooker/Manual" button and set the timer for 3 minutes on HIGH pressure.

Cut the leaves and excess stem from the bottom of the cauliflower. Wash the outside and inside the crevices as best as you can. Dry the surface well with a paper towel or a kitchen towel.

Put the water in the inner pot and place the trivet inside. Place the cauliflower on the trivet, close the lid tightly and move the steam release handle to "Sealing."

Preheat the oven at 550°F (288°C) or at the highest temperature your oven heats up to. Do not use the broiler. Place a sheet of parchment paper on a cookie sheet. Mix the melted butter, garlic, sea salt and black pepper in a small mixing bowl, and set aside.

When you hear the beeping sound indicating that the Instant Pot timer has ended, carefully turn the steam release handle to the "Venting" position for the steam to escape and the float valve to drop down. Press "Cancel," and open the lid. Carefully lift the trivet out and place the cauliflower on the lined cookie sheet. Dab and dry the surface with a clean kitchen towel or paper towel. With a pastry brush, liberally coat the cauliflower with the garlic butter.

Place the cookie sheet with the cauliflower in the middle rack of the preheated oven and roast for 5 minutes or until the cauliflower is golden brown. Drizzle on any remaining garlic butter, sprinkle with the parsley and serve immediately.

*Nutrition:* Per Serving: 140 calories; 12g fat; 3g protein; 8g total carbohydrate; 4g dietary fiber

# Buffalo Cauli Bites

This is a vegetable rendition of Buffalo chicken wings, and they are still finger-licking good without the greasy deep-fried taste. Cook them fast in the Instant Pot, finish them off in the oven, and they will be better than deep fried.

*Cooking Time: 0 minutes // Servings: 4*

1 head cauliflower, cut into florets

1 cup (240 ml) water

1 cup (223 g) mayonnaise

⅓ cup (80 g) full-fat coconut milk yogurt

1 tsp garlic powder

1 tsp onion powder

½ tsp sea salt

1 tsp apple cider vinegar (ACV)

1 tsp dried dill

4 tbsp (60 ml) melted butter, divided

3 tbsp (45 ml) hot sauce, or more as needed

1 tsp tapioca flour

1 carrot, cut into 3-inch (7.5-cm) sticks

2 celery stalks, cut into 3-inch (7.5-cm) pieces

Turn on the Instant Pot by pressing the "Pressure Cooker/Manual" button and set the timer for "0" minutes on HIGH pressure.

Cut and discard the outer leaves and cut the cauliflower into florets. Put the water in the inner pot and place the steamer basket inside. Put the florets in the steamer basket and close the lid tightly. Move the steam release handle to "Sealing."

In a small mixing bowl, mix the mayo, coconut milk yogurt, garlic powder, onion powder, sea salt, ACV and dill and refrigerate. Turn on the oven to broil.

When you hear the beeping sound indicating that the time has ended, carefully turn the steam release handle to the "Venting" position for the steam to escape and the float valve to drop down. Press "Cancel" and open the lid carefully.

In a small saucepan, combine the melted butter, hot sauce and tapioca flour and stir to thicken. Transfer the florets from the steamer basket inside the inner pot to a large mixing bowl and coat the florets well with the hot sauce. Spread the cauli bites on a roasting pan, and place under the broiler for 1 to 2 minutes or until the cauli bites are browned.

Take the ranch dressing out of the refrigerator. Serve the Buffalo Cauli Bites and carrot and celery sticks with the ranch dressing.

*Nutrition:* Per Serving: 563 calories; 59g fat; 5g protein; 13g total carbohydrate; 5g dietary fiber

# Noodle-Free Lasagna

Love lasagna but can't have the noodles? Don't worry. I've got your back. This Noodle-Free Lasagna will get you full without the carbs. And it's so much easier to make in the Instant Pot, too! The gooey cheese and ground beef will put a smile on your face.

*Cooking Time: 15 minutes // Servings: 4*

1 tbsp (15 ml) extra-virgin olive oil (EVOO)

1 small onion, diced

3 cloves garlic, minced

1 lb (450 g) ground beef

28 oz (790 g) can crushed tomatoes

2 tbsp (32 g) tomato paste

¼ tsp sea salt

¼ tsp black pepper

1 tsp dried basil

1 tbsp (4 g) dried parsley

1 tsp dried oregano

1 large egg

1½ cups (187 g) ricotta cheese

½ cup (91 g) grated Parmesan cheese

2 cups (226 g) shredded mozzarella cheese, divided

1 cup (240 ml) water

¼ cup (30 g) chopped fresh flat leaf parsley, for garnish

Turn on the Instant Pot by pressing "Sauté" and set to "More." Insert the inner pot and when the panel says "Hot," add the EVOO.

When the oil is hot, add the onion and garlic and sauté for 2 minutes or until the onion is soft. Add the ground beef and sauté for 3 minutes or until the meat is no longer pink. Drain the grease and add the crushed tomatoes, tomato paste, sea salt, black pepper and the herbs and mix. Remove the beef sauce to a large mixing bowl and set aside. Press "Cancel."

In a medium-sized mixing bowl, beat the egg. Add the ricotta cheese, Parmesan cheese and 1 cup (113 g) of mozzarella cheese, and mix.

In a deep casserole dish big enough to fit in the Instant Pot, layer the bottom with the beef sauce, then the cheese mixture, more beef sauce, then ½ cup (57 g) of mozzarella cheese, then more sauce, the rest of the cheese mixture and top with the rest of the mozzarella cheese. Loosely cover with aluminum foil.

Put the water in the inner pot and place the trivet inside. Lower the casserole dish on the trivet. Close the lid tightly and move the steam release handle to "Sealing."

Press the "Pressure Cooker/Manual" button and set the timer for 10 minutes on HIGH pressure. When the timer goes off, allow the Instant Pot to cool down naturally until the float valve drops down and you can open the lid. Press "Cancel." Remove the casserole dish and let it rest for 5 minutes, uncovered. If there's liquid on top, gently dab it with a paper towel. Divide the lasagna into 4 shallow bowls, garnish with the parsley and serve immediately.

*Nutrition:* Per Serving: 707 calories; 56g fat; 41g protein; 9g total carbohydrate; 2g dietary fiber

# Nourishing Cauli Mash

When I made this for my family, they honestly didn't know that this wasn't mashed potatoes. And my husband is a typical "meat and potatoes" kinda guy. Make this version. Seriously. You won't ever want to go back to making mashed potatoes again.

*Cooking Time: 5 minutes // Servings: 4*

1 head cauliflower

½ cup (120 ml) water

2 tbsp (30 ml) full-fat heavy whipping cream

2 tbsp (31 g) cream cheese

2 tbsp (12 g) collagen peptide powder

¼ tsp sea salt

1 tbsp (15 g) butter

¼ cup (30 g) chopped fresh flat leaf parsley

Turn on the Instant Pot by pressing the "Pressure Cooker/Manual" button and set the timer for "0" minutes on HIGH pressure.

Cut and discard the outer leaves and cut the cauliflower into florets. Put the water in the inner pot and place the steamer basket inside. Put the florets in the steamer basket and close the lid tightly. Move the steam release handle to "Sealing."

In a small mixing bowl, mix the heavy cream, cream cheese, collagen peptide powder and sea salt and set aside.

When you hear the beeping sound indicating that the time has ended, carefully turn the steam release handle to the "Venting" position for the steam to escape and the float valve to drop down. Open the lid carefully and remove the steamer basket and the florets. Pour out the water and put the florets back in the inner pot. The Instant Pot should be on "Warm." Add the butter and the cream mixture. Using an immersion blender, blend until smooth. Add more cream if needed. Press "Cancel," and serve immediately with the fresh parsley as a garnish.

*Nutrition:* Per Serving: 114 calories; 8g fat; 4g protein; 8g total carbohydrate; 4g dietary fiber

# Un-Guilty Pleasures

I was thrilled to learn that the Instant Pot is not just for pot roasts and chicken soup— it also makes desserts and drinks! Here are just a few samples of un-guilty treats you can make that will curb your sweet tooth without compromising the glycemic index. Chocolate Lava Cake (page 171) only takes minutes to make, but allow one day for the Espresso Cheesecake (page 168) since it will take a day for the cheesecake to get firm.

# Espresso Mocha Cheesecake

Cheesecake in the Instant Pot? Of course! And it makes it better than in the oven! Add some coffee, chocolate and raspberries, and who says you can't eat good food on Keto? Not me!

*Cooking Time: 35 minutes // Servings: 8*

1 cup (98 g) extra fine blanched almond flour

½ cup plus 2 tbsp (150 g) dry sweetener granules, divided (I use Swerve)

3 tbsp (21 g) espresso powder, divided

2 tbsp (30 g) butter

16 oz (450 g) cream cheese

1 egg

½ cup (120 ml) full-fat heavy cream

1 cup (240 ml) water

6 oz (170 g) dark chocolate (at least 80% cacao)

8 oz (227 g) full-fat heavy whipping cream

1 pint (75 g) raspberries

In a small mixing bowl, combine the almond flour, 2 tablespoons (30 g) of dry sweetener granules, 1 tablespoon (7 g) of espresso powder and the butter. The mixture should be wet, like modeling clay. Line the bottom of the springform pan with parchment paper. Press the almond flour dough flat on the bottom and about 1 inch (2.5 cm) on the sides. Set aside.

In a food processor or using a handheld mixer, mix the cream cheese, egg, heavy cream, remaining dry sweetener granules and remaining espresso powder until smooth. Pour the cream cheese mixture into the springform pan. Loosely cover with aluminum foil.

Put the water in the inner pot and place the trivet inside. Close the lid tightly and move the steam release handle to "Sealing." Turn on the Instant Pot by pressing the "Pressure Cooker/Manual" button and set the timer for 35 minutes on HIGH pressure. Close the lid tightly and move the steam release handle to "Sealing."

When the timer ends, you will hear a beeping sound. Allow the Instant Pot to cool down naturally until the float valve drops down. Press "Cancel," and open the lid. Remove the springform pan and place it on a cooling rack for 2 to 3 hours or until it reaches room temperature. At this point, the cheesecake will be jiggly. Refrigerate overnight.

The next day, melt the chocolate and heavy whipping cream in the double boiler. Cool for 15 minutes and drizzle on top of the cheesecake, allowing the chocolate to drip down the sides. Add the raspberries on top of the cheesecake before serving.

*Nutrition:* Per Serving: 586 calories; 54g fat; 12g protein; 15g total carbohydrate; 4g dietary fiber

# Chocolate Lava Cake

Once in a while, you need a little treat, and this quick and easy chocolate cake is just what you need. And you won't have to feel guilty when you indulge on this decadent but sugar-free cake!

*Cooking Time: 5 minutes // Servings: 2*

1 large egg

4 tbsp (22 g) unsweetened raw cocoa powder

2 tbsp (30 g) dry sweetener granules (I use Swerve)

2 tbsp (12 g) extra fine blanched almond flour

2 tbsp (30 ml) full-fat heavy cream

1 tsp vanilla extract

½ tsp baking powder

Pinch of sea salt

2 oz (56 g) dark chocolate (at least 80% cacao), cut into chunks

½ cup (120 ml) water

½ cup (120 ml) full-fat heavy whipping cream (optional)

Turn on the Instant Pot by pressing the "Pressure Cooker/Manual" button and set the timer for 5 minutes on HIGH pressure.

In a small mixing bowl, beat the egg and add the cocoa powder, dry sweetener, almond flour, heavy cream, vanilla extract, baking powder and sea salt. Transfer half of the batter into a small ovenproof bowl, add the dark chocolate pieces and then the rest of the batter. Loosely cover with aluminum foil. Put the water in the inner pot and place the trivet inside. Place the bowl on the trivet.

Close the lid rightly and move the steam release handle to "Sealing." If using, place the heavy whipping cream in a small mixing bowl and whisk until soft peaks form and set aside.

When the timer ends, you will hear a beeping sound. Allow the Instant Pot to cool down naturally until the float valve drops down. Press "Cancel," and open the lid. Remove the bowl, uncover, top with the whipped cream, if using, and serve immediately.

---

*Nutrition:* Per Serving: 288 calories; 24g fat; 17g protein; 8g total carbohydrate; 6g dietary fiber

# Pine Nut Mousse

My Italian friend gave me this recipe years ago and I remember thinking how sweet it was. In fact, it was too sweet to enjoy the pine nut flavors. So, I re-created this Keto version, made it in the Instant Pot as a mousse and I love it. But shhhh…don't tell her.

*Cooking Time: 35 minutes // Servings: 8*

1 tbsp (15 g) butter

1¼ cups (170 g) pine nuts

1¼ cups (300 ml) full-fat heavy cream

2 large eggs

1 tsp vanilla extract

1 cup (240 g) dry sweetener granules, reserve 1 tbsp (12 g) (I use Swerve)

1 cup (240 ml) water

1 cup (240 ml) full-fat heavy whipping cream

Turn on the Instant Pot by pressing the "Pressure Cooker/Manual" button and set the timer for 35 minutes on HIGH pressure.

Butter the bottom and the side of a pie pan or a casserole dish that can fit in the Instant Pot and set aside.

In a blender or a food processor, blend the pine nuts and heavy cream. Add the eggs, vanilla extract and dry sweetener and pulse a few times to incorporate. Pour the batter into the pan and loosely cover with aluminum foil. Pour the water in the inner pot and place the trivet inside. Place the pan on top of the trivet.

Close the lid tightly and move the steam release handle to "Sealing."

In a small mixing bowl, whisk the heavy whipping cream and 1 tablespoon (12 g) of dry sweetener until a soft peak forms.

When the timer ends, you will hear a beeping sound. Allow the Instant Pot to cool down naturally until the float valve drops down. Press "Cancel" and open the lid. Serve immediately with whipped cream on top.

---

*Nutrition:* Per Serving: 185 calories; 19g fat; 3g protein; 2g total carbohydrate; trace dietary fiber

---

# Buttered Popcorn

I'm including this "controversial" popcorn recipe because there are people who are on Keto for weight loss. And if they are watching their carb intake, they can indulge on a cup of popcorn occasionally without going over their daily allowance. But if you're on Keto for specific health reasons, obviously it's best to skip this grain. I wanted to share how easy it is to make healthy popcorn in the Instant Pot and how you can avoid the GMO popcorn on the market by buying organic kernels. I won't make popcorn any other way now.

*Cooking Time: 5 minutes // Servings: 10*

**3 tbsp (45 ml) coconut or avocado oil**

**½ cup (113 g) organic popcorn kernels**

**1 tbsp (15 g) butter**

**1 tsp sea salt**

Turn on the Instant Pot by pressing "Sauté" and set to "More." Insert the inner pot to Instant Pot and pour the oil inside. Add the popcorn kernels and make sure all of the kernels are coated with oil. Close the pot with a glass lid. If you don't have the Instant Pot glass lid, find a tight-fitting lid you might already have from the cabinet. In about 2 to 3 minutes, the popcorn kernels will start to pop.

When about ⅔ of the popcorn is popped, press "Cancel," and take the pot WITH the lid out. Add the butter to the bottom of the pot, close the lid and shake to mix. Sprinkle with sea salt and serve!

*Nutrition:* Per Serving: 78 calories; 6g fat; 1g protein; 8g total carbohydrate; 2g dietary fiber

# Approximate Chai Tea

Approximate measurements of ingredients are what this recipe calls for. There is no right or wrong way to make this tea. The proportions are according to what you like and you can adjust them as you please. If you've never made chai tea from scratch, start with the lowest amount first and build up. What's amazing about making tea in the Instant Pot are the deeper flavors that it brings out.

*Cooking Time: // Servings: 4*

4 cups (960 ml) water

10–20 cardamom seeds in pods

4 tsp (3 g) loose Darjeeling tea leaves

10–20 whole cloves

3 tbsp (18 g) fennel seeds

1 (3-inch [7.5-cm]) stick cinnamon

1 tsp fresh ground black pepper

1 cup (240 ml) full-fat coconut milk (optional)

⅓ cup (80 g) sweetener of your choice (optional)

Turn on the Instant Pot by pressing "Sauté" and set to "More." Insert the inner pot and wait until the panel says "Hot."

Add the cold filtered water to the inner pot. Crush the cardamom pods and add all of the shells and seeds into the boiling water. Let the mixture boil for about 30 seconds. Then, add the rest of the spices and tea leaves. Close the lid tightly and move the steam release handle to "Sealing." Press the "Pressure Cooker/Manual" button and set the timer for "0" minutes on HIGH pressure.

When you hear the beeping sound indicating that the time has ended, carefully turn the steam release handle to the "Venting" position for the steam to escape and the float valve to drop down. Press "Cancel," and open the lid carefully. Add the milk and sweetener, if using. Strain and serve immediately.

---

*Nutrition:* Per Serving: 623 calories; 60g fat; 8g protein; 25g total carbohydrate; 14g dietary fiber if using milk and sweetener

---

# Immune-Boosting Ginger Tea

When your immune system is on the fritz, the first thing you reach for is a soothing, warm drink. This herbal tea will boost your immune system right back up and get you on the road to recovery fast! And it takes no time to make it in the Instant Pot while sealing in all the goodness during brewing!

*Cooking Time: 1 minute // Servings: 4*

4 cups (960 ml) water

1 (3-inch [7.5-cm]) piece fresh ginger, sliced

3 whole cloves

1 (1-inch [2.5-cm]) stick cinnamon

3 jujubes (optional)

2 lemons, peels from 1 lemon, slices from 1 lemon

1 tbsp (2 g) whole stevia leaves or sweetener of your choice (optional)

Turn on the Instant Pot by pressing "Sauté" and set to "More." Insert the inner pot and wait until the panel says "Hot."

Add the cold filtered water to the inner pot. Add the ginger, cloves, cinnamon stick, jujubes (if using), peels from one lemon and stevia leaves (if using). Close the lid tightly and move the steam release handle to "Sealing." Press the "Pressure Cooker/Manual" button and set the timer for "0" minutes on HIGH pressure.

When you hear the beeping sound indicating that the time has ended, carefully turn the steam release handle to the "Venting" position for the steam to escape and the float valve to drop down. Press "Cancel," and open the lid carefully. Strain, add one lemon slice per cup and serve immediately.

*Nutrition:* Per Serving: 29 calories; 1g fat; 1g protein; 9g total carbohydrate; 3g dietary fiber

# Golden Spice Milk

Turmeric is a wonderful anti-inflammatory spice. I don't think we use it enough so I like drinking this warm milk as a supplement. Get the benefits from turmeric by brewing this golden milk in the Instant Pot fast. I think the coconut milk sweetens it enough but you can add your favorite sweetener, if needed.

*Cooking Time: 1 minute // Servings: 4*

4 cups (960 ml) water

1 (3-inch [7.5-cm]) piece whole turmeric, sliced

1 (2-inch [5-cm]) piece ginger, sliced

1 tsp black peppercorn

1 (1-inch [2.5-cm]) stick cinnamon

3 whole cloves

1 cup (240 ml) full-fat coconut milk

1 tbsp (15 g) sweetener of your choice (optional)

1 tsp cinnamon, ground, for garnish

Turn on the Instant Pot by pressing "Sauté" and set to "More." Insert the inner pot. Add the cold filtered water, turmeric, ginger, peppercorn, cinnamon stick and cloves. Close the lid tightly and move the steam release handle to "Sealing." Press the "Pressure Cooker/Manual" button and set the timer for "0" minutes on HIGH pressure.

When you hear the beeping sound indicating that the time has ended, carefully turn the steam release handle to the "Venting" position for the steam to escape and the float valve to drop down. Press "Cancel," and open the lid carefully. Add the coconut milk and sweetener, if using. Strain and garnish with ground cinnamon and serve immediately.

*Nutrition:* Per Serving: 160 calories; 15g fat; 2g protein; 8g total carbohydrate; 3g dietary fiber

# Acknowledgments

Writing a cookbook requires a tribe of supporters: dishwashers, taste testers, copywriters and cheerleaders. Without these incredible supporters in my life, I couldn't have written a second cookbook!

My husband: Thank you for being the taste tester and overindulging on creamy and cheesy foods that you don't usually eat, in the name of trying a Ketogenic diet. And of course, I appreciate your brutal honesty in giving me the thumbs up or thumbs down on whether a recipe should be included in this book or not. I'm thrilled that at least 75 of them got your approval.

My children: Once again, you came through in trying all the recipes, whether you wanted to or not. And trusting my telling you that it's okay to eat new foods despite your allergies. How great is it that you discovered you can manage some dairy and eggs now! I hope my next cookbook will be using ingredients you couldn't eat before being on Keto.

Friends from all walks of life who continuously support me and give me strength: Lisa MarcAurele, Cristina Curp and Heather Rushin for sharing your Keto journeys. Hayley Ryczek for accepting me into the Bloggers Writing Cookbooks group and sharing your publishing experiences. I couldn't have written this special book without your support. And friends near and far, I love you for checking in regularly and encouraging me, keeping me company and promising to buy my books. I love you all!

My photographer/confidant Donna Crouse: I couldn't have written another cookbook without your uber-creative ideas and cheerleading. I am so honored that you accepted my request to photograph my work again. I can't thank you enough for making my recipes come to life more beautifully than I could ever have imagined.

Page Street Publishing, Marissa, Meg and William: Once again, you had the confidence in me to write another cookbook! I am honored to be in that rare category of cookbook authors and I cannot thank you enough. You made me cry the first time I saw the beautiful cover of the book.

To my loyal readers and followers: Your constant support makes me do what I do. Your demand for learning about holistic health and real food recipes keeps me striving to be better. Thank you so much for your love!

# About the Author

Dr. Karen Lee is an accomplished holistic practitioner with a Doctor of Chiropractic degree and an Acupuncture and Oriental Medicine Fellow. Dr. Karen treated patients with various ailments with standard chiropractic care, acupuncture, nutrition therapy and mind body medicine before she retired.

Dr. Karen started writing about holistic health and real food recipes on drkarenslee.com after helping her children with numerous food allergies and sensitivities. She is confident that many illnesses can be prevented or reversed with real food, proper nutrition, supplements and stress management. She also believes that many of the health struggles can be managed effectively by adopting a whole food, real ingredient eating habit as a lifestyle and not as a mere temporary "diet." Dr. Karen shares allergy-friendly, Keto and Asian Paleo recipes that have helped many people across the world on her website drkarenslee.com. You can find her popular cookbook, *Paleo Cooking with Your Air Fryer*, on Amazon and everywhere else books are sold. You can find her as @drkarenslee on social media.

# Index